PRESCRIPTION FOR TODAY'S MISSIONARY

Foreword

It has been a pleasure to read the manuscript of this book written by a friend of many years, dealing as it does with a subject of vital importance, especially in the missionary sphere. There is sane guidance here for both the young aspirant to effectiveness in Christian work and the seasoned warrior.

The book is concerned not so much with opinions as with principles, and principles are 'fundamental truths on which others are founded, or from which they spring'. This ensures for it a more than temporary relevance. It abounds with flashes of insight into Scripture, pungently expressed, which are the outcome of meditation and keen observation. Both Biblical and contemporary biography have been freely drawn upon.

The missionary flavour does not detract from the value of the book to leaders, whether potential or prospective, in other spheres of service. Naturally a missionary in Japan will draw largely on Japanese sources for his illustrative material, but most of what is written is applicable to the general missionary situation.

There is much sound and practical wisdom which the author has tested in the crucible of his considerable missionary experience. A glance at the chapter headings reveals that many aspects of Christian leadership come under review, and there is a considerable amount of material this writer has not read elsewhere. I commend it most warmly to all who desire to be their best in God's service.

Auckland
New Zealand

J. OSWALD SANDERS

Contents

Preface

Recently I received a letter from a Japanese missionary society asking if I would send my mission's 'prescription for missionary'. The writer said they intended to use it for reference when they made 'their prescription for missionary'. The quaint misuse of a medical and legal term provoked both fun and serious reflection. What is a missionary anyway?

Even the new concept of the non-professional missionary calls for some realistic thinking and clear-cut definition. Going abroad as a non-professional missionary does not guarantee that we will not become 'professional'. Our constant prayer is that we will be kept from just that. We merely want to be witnessing Christians living in a foreign culture. This does not, of course, mean that we have any inclination to leave the mission society to which we belong. Professionalism or non-professionalism can be a matter largely of heart and mind rather than that of relationship with some organisation.

A rapidly shrinking globe may do something to remove the mistaken image of the missionary as being something specially 'other'. In point of fact, every Christian is a missionary. If we belong to the Lord then we are His sent ones to the society where He has placed us—

a society that can be thoroughly alien and utterly foreign as far as the Kingdom of God is concerned. In that society we can be good missionaries or bad missionaries, witnessing missionaries or non-witnessing missionaries, faithful missionaries or unfaithful missionaries, but we are missionaries in a broad scriptural sense. It follows therefore if we are not faithful and witness where we are, then we will not be faithful nor witness in any other culture we care to go to, or 'feel called to'. For this reason, much of what I write here will be seen to apply to every Christian.

Today, however, it is true that the role of the overseas missionary is tremendously challenging and exciting in its call to adaption and flexibility. The phenomenal growth of the Christian Church in Latin America and parts of South-east Asia has stretched the capacity of specialist (foreign) teachers to the utmost. With it has come a melting of denominational incidentals. The ubiquitous gramophone record is speedily being replaced by the cassette tape-recorder that is finding its way into the remotest parts of the Far East and other places not readily approachable to regular ministry by national nor foreigner.

Radio ministry itself is making more demands than thoroughly trained personnel can rise to, and the special courses in a seminary like that of Hong Kong are all too few and far between. Writing courses for nationals are becoming increasingly common as literacy rates rise and nationals are awakened to see the need of reading material for their own mentally starved people. Gospel broadsheets in the vernacular are being distributed in many countries in their hundreds of thousands. Correspondence courses arising from this and the expanding radio ministry call for ever increasing staff.

Theological extension courses for an expanding rural church have come to stay. Missionaries' training centres for nationals are beginning to appear as the initiative for pioneer missionary work is increasingly shared by the nationals themselves. This very training offers a satisfying ministry for the veteran foreign missionary. Positions for foreign teachers in the mushrooming educational programmes of the new nations are often available and just why any robust Christian teacher should retire at home with this exciting and demanding ministry available is a puzzle to me! Whether they are to be called non-professional missionaries, or Christians serving the Lord overseas, it matters little. In some cases, of course, the missionary has to be in mufti—he is a missionary incognito, for he is deliberately going to a staff position in a foreign university or some such post with the determined intention of winning individuals to the Saviour, but in a country where any organised witness is strictly forbidden. This kind of witness is not only exciting and dangerous, but can be very lonely indeed, for the usual avenues of two-way prayer communication with friends at home are impossible.

All these and other avenues of witness have challenged missionary leaders to rethink their commission, and mission societies to regroup and amalgamate where ministry can helpfully overlap. It has led some to update their requirements and to reword their principles to suit the expanding ministries of the hour.

But the most important factors in effective missionary life and ministry remain unchanged, namely, what kind of a person ought the missionary to be? What is the significance of God's call to that kind of leadership? The moral and spiritual requisites have not changed from apostolic times. Indeed, the very sophistication and peculiar demands of our times will test whether or not we do have the essentials that made the apostles the missionaries they were.

This book is an attempt therefore to examine some of those essentials against the background of missionary life in one of the world's most cultured and advanced civilisations.

It remains for me to thank the several missionary

friends who have helped with the typing of the manuscript from time to time and to express regret that the
book was not completed before a very wonderful mother
went to her reward. To her memory, this book is dedicated.

K.S.R.

I

The Call of Abraham

By popular definition, a leader is one who says what everyone else is saying—in the loudest voice! There is a tendency today to indulge in hero-worship of popular characters: football players and pop-singers with a fan-mail from thousands of teenagers; successful writers and musicians; prominent figures in the academic world.

Among Christians there is often the feeling that the support of someone in the public eye is essential to the success of some cause. Given a Nobel Prize-winner, all will be fine. In choosing leaders, also, the same factors which contribute to a person's social prestige may be allowed to sway things: a dominating manner, influence in certain spheres, oratorical skill, intellectual or athletic prowess.

All this was summed up a few years ago by M. S. Foote in an article on leadership: 'We, who live in an age of the cult of personality, can be too easily influenced, both in the choice of leaders and in the giving of our allegiance, by secular reputation, by powerful personalities, by those who have much to display in the shop-window.'[1]

Although God may choose for His own purposes a man like Paul with natural talents for leadership, and may richly bless his ministry, the possession of natural

13

wisdom does not automatically qualify the Christian for service. Paul himself, writing to the Corinthian believers about the call of God (1 Cor. 1:17–2:16), sets it against the popular opinion of the great and the praiseworthy. In 1:20 he speaks of 'the wise man', i.e. the thinker, 'the scribe', i.e. the writer, and 'the debater', i.e. the orator or the fast talker. These undoubtedly were the 'gifted' to the Corinthian Greeks. In some of these talents Paul may have outshone many of his contemporaries, but he had the discernment to know that they were not the key to open the mysteries of revelation (2:7), nor did they lend persuasive powers to his efforts to convince others of its verity (2:3–5).

Even among those who were mature (2:6), presumably those of like moral and intellectual background, Paul could see that true wisdom was not the product of the academic disciplines of his day, but was the fruit of the Spirit controlling the life (2:10). So there was no ground for boasting in one's own skills, but only in the power of Christ.

The Corinthians could find an illustration of this principle in their own lives ('consider your call, brethren . . .', 1:26). Not many were wise, yet they were 'called to be saints' (1:2). The Christian is called initially to repentance and faith, and we may take this to be the prime meaning here. But with this call is involved a wider call to the whole of God's purposes, revealed gradually as the Christian 'grows in grace'. To each individual the call will be different and there may be one or many—to missionary service, to Sunday school teaching, to a new job, to university or college. From our subsequent studies of some of the leaders in the Bible we shall see some of the principles on which God works to bring His children to a stage at which they can be used by Him—as responsible Christians with a variety of commitments according to their spiritual gifts.

For our first example, let us look at the life of Abraham as described in Genesis 12–22. As we study God's dealings with him, various points emerge :

a. The call came to Abraham while he was still immature. Abraham lived originally in Ur of the Chaldees where, according to Joshua 24 : 2, 3, his family were idolaters. How he grew in sensitiveness to God with that background is not recorded. But we are told that he heard God's voice and, though limited in directions to the first major step, as is often the case in a walk with God, it was explicit enough for the initial act of obedience. God can have His Moses in an Egyptian court, His Saul in the bosom of the Sanhedrin and His Luther in the cloisters of the papal church and speak to each in no uncertain voice. It is the measure of Abraham's greatness that, though more limited in knowledge than any of these, he still stepped out in the obedience of faith. Admittedly, and perhaps for our comfort, his initial obedience appears to have been imperfect and with some reservations.

Genesis 11 : 29–32 records the first major move towards the promised Canaan. We gather from Acts 7 : 2–4 that Abraham was told to leave his family as well as his country. But Terah evidently refused to part with his cherished eldest son and, rather than permit a break-up of the ancestral home, decided to go with him on this 'mad quest'. In the East, the loss of the eldest son as the future head of the clan is no small affair. Terah had to die in Haran before Abraham set his face towards the promised land. After Terah's death God once more commanded that Abraham must leave all kindred as well as his country behind him (Gen. 12 : 1). But a few verses later we hear that Lot his nephew was with him! He proved to be no small thorn in his uncle's flesh and it is salutary to notice that only after Lot separated from

Abraham (13 : 14) did the Lord speak to Abraham again about the possession of Canaan.

Our formative years are marked with tremendous potential for good or evil.

> If a man is leadership material, he is a marked man. Every characteristic, every talent, the nature of his pleasures, indulgences, failings, his peculiar idiosyncrasies and besetting sins, are all mercilessly noted by the enemy for exploitation. He is going to be the target of a most subtle and crafty attack whose director is the father of lies. No trouble will be spared to counter or maim him. If he can only be deflected in these early days one hair's breath from the straight course, a few years will take him wide of the goal; if he can now effectively be dealt with, he may later be left alone to pursue his devious course unmolested.[2]

Many a young Christian is deflected by unwise partnerships or contracts that prejudice the whole future course of his life. Even when there is some sense of God's call to the foreign field or other service, for example, marriages are frequently contracted too hastily. Though the partner may even be a keen Christian, if there is never a corresponding sense of call, what should have been a fruitful happy Christian home is clouded by a felt loss of heart-rest at missing God's best.

b. The call to Abraham came in great ignorance of detail. It is part of the tutelage in God's school of faith that we cannot question the possible results of obedience; 'he went out, not knowing where he was to go' (Heb. 11 : 8). If he did not know, picture his attempts to answer the anxious or mocking enquiries of friends and relatives. Faith expresses itself best in acts of obedience. To try to explain the mystery of God's dealings with us, especially to non-Christians, is very much like trying to describe the beauties of a sunset to a man born blind.

Nothing is said of how Abraham reasoned either with his relatives or with his own heart, but he had to get alone with God. A well-organised society had to be exchanged for the solitary life of the nomad, where details mattered less than the broad sweep of God's majestic purposes. Dr A. W. Tozer suggests that God never spoke to Abraham in the presence of other men. Actually there seems to have been a 'desert' experience in the lives of many of God's chosen leaders. Surely King Uzziah must have been the centre of Isaiah's hopes for some great revival in Judah, and then he was smitten down. But it is at this point that Isaiah in biography declares, 'In the year that King Uzziah died I saw the Lord . . .'. The death of human hopes became the birthplace of a new dedication and a larger ministry.

'The word of God came to John the son of Zechariah in the wilderness . . .' (Luke 3 : 1–3). What an inglorious bevy of political and ecclesiastical leaders the Lord bypassed to get to John! Read it for yourself. He did not get his 'fire-words' from any of that day's theological pedants. Paul went to Arabia, not very far from the place where Moses must have spent his forty years learning just how small he was. Perhaps it was there that all Paul had learnt of the law at the feet of Gamaliel became so thoroughly fused with his new-found life in Christ.

If a Christian, specially a leader, is to see beyond the present details, be they favourable or unfavourable, it is essential that he maintain a solitary walk with God. He will be caught up in the maelstrom of conflicting ideologies and loaded questions. The greater his gifts, the more frequent the temptation to trust his native capacity. If he has been largely sustained by group stimulus and has a growing skill as cheer-leader, a sudden change of environment or isolation will reveal a sad lack of reality and leave him wide open to satanic discouragement. Pity the Christian who is only a spiritual mollusc. He clings to what is near and substantial.

If we fail to learn how to walk with God, whether in isolation or in the crowd, a training at Bible or theological college will simply fill the mind with spiritual clichés that may later be parroted with the utmost precision, but be as ineffective as Gehazi's borrowed rod. In this age of noise where concentration is difficult, packeted capsules of spiritual vitamins may superficially flush the skin but will put nothing substantial in the spiritual stomach. And that is what we march on! Details will not irritate the man who walks alone with God, nor will he be dependent upon them for stimulus. His convictions will find their birth in the secret place, and as his range of leadership increases he will find that his walk is increasingly a lonely one, a prerogative and a paradox that is not without its cost for any true man of God.

When some fresh call comes to us, our immediate reaction is often to ask about the implications. Yes, we *do* want the details; but the call comes to us seemingly in a vague way as part of the discipline of discipleship. We will be trusted with even less of the sensory as we are able to bear the loss. I have on occasion trembled to think how easily, apparently, I could have missed the way. How quiet was the voice! Insistent, yes, but if so much was involved, why did He not shout at me? Elijah would probably remind us that neither wind, earthquake nor fire was as insistent as the still small voice.

c. For Abraham, the call came progressively and unfolded as he was able to appreciate its meaning. The initial test must have seemed enormous, but it was simple compared with the complexity of the tests to follow. It is part of the outworking of the call that tests proceed from the small to the large and from the simple to the complex. We progress from problem to problem. Or, to quote J. O. Sanders, we find that God's tests can be His votes of confidence.

That confidence seems sadly misplaced when we see Abraham turn down to Egypt because of famine and even more so when he lies about his wife to protect his own skin (Gen. 12:10–13:1). 'Even a lie is convenient', runs the Japanese proverb, but even if his was a so-called half-truth, he nearly lost Sarah in the process, and it hardly commended him as a servant of the living God to a heathen court.

Some missionaries are known to run and not grow weary, but when it comes to walking they faint away. The initial call finds them radiantly responsive. There seems to be a joy in sacrificing for Jesus's sake, but then as the initially spectacular gives way to the common-place, horrid little mannerisms and temporarily hidden attitudes become all too apparent and mar the person's usefulness. It is the way we react to the small tests at the beginning that determines how we will fare in some major crisis later. If we invariably choose easy options at college and never cudgel our brains with something beyond our present fancied powers, we can set a pattern of irresponsibility that is difficult to break.

How we instinctively react to small moral tests in-volving scrupulous honesty will give a fair indication of later faithfulness in very grave decisions. Do I im-mediately repay the shopkeeper when he makes a mis-take in my favour in the change? Or do I congratulate myself on some unsought profit? The thing that proves our sincerity and impresses the unbeliever is when the Christian is honest at great cost to himself when no one would ordinarily know if he was not.

Abraham, publicly rebuked to his shame, was wise enough to return to the place of his earlier trysts with God (Gen. 13:3, 4). According to the proverb, the just man falls seven times but rises again. He is known by his rising up rather than by his sitting down. J. O. Sanders has pointed out that Abraham was not judged by his occasional failure but by the tenor of his life which gave way more and more to obedience and faith.

Genesis 13–15 records the next major test in which that tenor was seen most unmistakably in Abraham's glorious victory over the god mammon. While Lot chose the rich plains in the valleys below, Abraham was content to walk the length and breadth of God's promises in a purer atmosphere. He anticipated Paul's lofty principles of Christian conduct when he refused to be mastered by what was legitimate and returned the proffered gift of the heathen king.

Here, too, we find our first reference to tithing (14:20), obviously something as fundamental to the divine economy as the sabbath or Lord's day, both predating the Ten Commandments by several hundred years. Tithing, or giving the tenth part of everything to God (Gen. 28:22), became part of the way of life for Israel (Lev. 27:30 4) and obligatory. It would seem from Paul's writings that, for the Christian, there is no place for tithing as a legal necessity; voluntary giving out of thankfulness has taken its place.

Nevertheless, at the very dawn of our Christian experience we need to claim absolute mastery over money by wisely and systematically giving it away. If not, it will master us. It is not how much I give to God as His, but how much I retain of His for myself. In other words, to tithe, whether it be with little or much, is proof that we recognise that all we have belongs to God and we are simply stewards of His largesse. We cannot be stewards of a few pence till we have given God the whole pound! The tithe is, therefore, the Christian's pledge that he is going to use the rest as though it did indeed belong to God and not to himself.

We are natural casuists when it comes to the control of the purse—'the last part of a man to be saved'. Christian workers both at home and abroad are not without the temptation of thinking that because they are in full-time work for God, all they receive is from the tithes of the Lord's people and they are living wholly for Him, and so why tithe it again? Even if the Lord were not in need of such acts of worship, it goes without saying that we never get to the place where *we* do not need this exercise. A sacrifice becomes an increasing joy as we are directed, often in extraordinary ways, to become the vehicles of the Lord's provision to others in real need.

Abraham's willingness to surrender his claim to material possessions was a preparation for a much keener test that involved the surrender of his dear child Isaac. The cost in any call of God is cumulative. The giving up of things is only kindergarten stuff compared with what He gently leads us into in the ultimate. The loss of 'things' can simply add to our mobility, as one missionary confessed when he lost all his! But ultimately, if we are to know the heart of the Father, we will be able to say of the very dearest thing He vouchsafed, 'It never was mine.'

To Abraham, the supreme test of his faith came through his affections. Genesis 15 records the Lord's promise that his offspring would one day bless the earth. There was neither child in sight nor within the realm of possibility.

The Lord seems to love to challenge us to the impossible when family and friends find it difficult not to laugh in unbelief. If *He* bids us come to Him across the water, then we can walk on it and be safe. When the disciples saw the thoughtless crowd (Mark 6:36, 37), they told Him to send them away, and His reply was, '*You* give them something to eat.' If He commands it, then it can be done. If there is even a remote possibility of the thing being done by human ingenuity, or of that happy concomitant of events that on occasion produces the rare and undefinable, then there is all the less room for faith. Perhaps this is why the Lord chose to keep His child waiting, for His delays have never been a denial. Genesis 16 records the altogether natural but fleshly expedient that has given rise to friction with Israel ever since. Ishmael. The Arab!

The Lord was weaning His servant from the tangible, but Abraham could not wait. How much of the Bible is taken up with the same sad sequence! Saul kicking his heels because Samuel would not appear just at the right psychological moment; his impatience lost him the kingdom. Moses thought he had buried his mistake, but forty years proved a long time to learn that you cannot hurry God's grindstone along. Nadab and Abihu, the sons of Aaron, could not wait for the high priesthood to come to one of them in natural succession but presumed to enter the holiest of all in what may have been the false courage of too much wine. Theirs proved to be a fiery sobering! Even when Jesus was walking in the shadow of the cross, the disciples were arguing among themselves about ringside seats in the coming kingdom. Only time could reveal the utter blindness of their motives and methods—the fullness of His time.

When young in the faith and in the first flush of our zeal, we tend to get impatient with the apparent inertia above us. We want things done, not tomorrow, but yesterday. Often our plans for a Bible college training are premature. The reality of our call needs to be proved in the rigours of the outdoors before it basks and flourishes in the warmth of a spiritual hot-house. The mission field, for example, is no place to take up elementary lessons in fighting entrenched idolatry and a venerable pagan society wholly at the mercy of Satan. We need to cut our spiritual teeth at home, and be weaned from the multitude of props that characterise a molly-coddled Christendom, before we can hope to make any adult impression in a land where we are going to be desperately lonely and perhaps the one solitary Christian among the hundred thousands. And that takes time.

Abraham had begged the Lord to consider Ishmael as a good second alternative (Gen. 17:18) but his affection for his natural-born child was no criterion for the fulfilment of God's lofty purposes. Worse was to come. Imagine the horror that Isaac, the direct gift of God, the very fulfilment of God's expressed purposes, should be offered up like a Canaanite child to Molech (Gen. 22 : 1–14). Yet the man who once had not wavered in unbelief did not now linger in disobedience. Perhaps before Sarah could dissuade him or even guess his intentions, he rose early in the morning and was off on a journey that took him closer to the heart of the Father than anyone before the Lamb Himself appeared. Indeed, it was Jesus Himself who finally answered the query of Isaac that day.

Perhaps the supreme test will always be in the realm of the affections. It was the criterion for Peter's restoration. It found Demas perverted. For Abraham, the progress had been from things to people, but what shall we say then when the test seems to be the very negation of God's expressed intention? Does God contradict Himself?

For us, it may never be a child that we have to place on the altar of God's good and perfect will. It may be our very call to the mission field. Geoffrey Bull in his book *God Holds the Key*, has touched on this so helpfully that we can do no better than reproduce the section as he wrote it :

He (Abraham) was pouring out the very fundamental of his life, yielding the centre of all his hopes, for ever abandoning to God the only channel of all His blessing to all generations. He was slaying his only boy for whom he had agonised, and in whom lay everything he had. Had I anything to give that was comparable in principle, to this? Something that was not just precious, but vital. Not the material incidentals but something utterly fundamental to me in the realm of the spirit, upon which the blessing even of others depended. Suddenly I knew that what I called 'my call' was precisely that to me. It had become indeed quite fundamental to me. I could not imagine life without it. My call had become the very life I lived. Somehow I had made it mine, when really it was always His, made it in a way, my 'only begotten son' which I loved more than anything else in the world, perhaps now I come to ponder it, even more than Christ. God's call had become my career. Thus, that which had been originally 'of God' could not be 'for God' because it had now become something 'for me'. His 'work' had become more than His will. The sense of His appointment more than the importance of His pleasure. His things more than Himself. . . .[3]

To every young Christian facing the unknown future, yet none the less conscious of an equally great and insistent command, there may come times of bewilderment, of wavering; times of alluring alternatives that make the good the enemy of the best; times when through lack of patience he cannot see the wisdom of His ways and is tempted to pull strings; but, again and again, there will be an altar.

With every fresh dedication, the cost will be swallowed up in the growing knowledge and appreciation of the wonder and perfection of His good and perfect will, and the fact that God relentlessly and gloriously commissions those whom He calls.

1. M. S. Foote, 'Christian Leadership', *Inter-Varsity* (Spring 1959), p. 12.

2. Mildred Cable and Francesca French, *Ambassadors for Christ* (Paternoster Press).

3. Geoffrey Bull, *God Holds the Key* (Hodder and Stoughton), p. 96.

The Call of Moses

In the call of Moses we find elements which are not likely to be duplicated in our lives today. He was disciplined to lead an enslaved nation not just to a physical freedom, but into a new sense of moral and spiritual destiny. Further, as promulgator and expounder of the law which commonly bears his own name, much of his teaching was preparatory and geared to a passing need. Although that law has never been annulled, and still needs to be taught as preparation for the gospel, the Lord Himself now writes it upon our hearts by the Holy Spirit. Thus James calls it the 'perfect law', the 'law of liberty', the 'royal law' (Jas. 1:25; 2:8); we now obey the law out of love for the Son of God and not out of fear of Sinai.

There are other elements in the leadership of Moses, however, that are of timeless value and still make him a leader whose faith and example we should follow. Heaven's own estimation of him should be incentive enough, for one day the redeemed are to sing the song both of Moses and of the Lamb (Rev. 15:3). We find Moses, now firmly in the promised land, together with Elijah, sharing with our Lord on the mount of transfiguration the secrets of His coming exodus (Matt. 17:3; Mark 9:4). On reflection, apart from our Lord Himself, has the Bible eulogised anyone so unstintingly as Moses? He in some peculiar way apart from symbol could speak to the Lord face to face. He was faithful in all his house and not least, in that curious parenthesis in Numbers 12:3, was called the meekest man on earth! It is profitable to follow, even if only in broadest outline, just how God made him the leader he became.

With Moses, the call to leadership was no 'impulse of a moment but the trend of a lifetime'. His very name, as one 'drawn out', though perhaps commemorative of his rescue from the Nile as a baby, surely was also prophetic of his future task in drawing out a whole nation from slavery to theocratic nationhood.

The discipline of applied diligence
Stephen tells us (Acts 7:22) that Moses was learned in all the wisdom of the Egyptians, a discipline that was not meant to add to the law later revealed to him, but surely to prepare his mind for all the sustained concentration and attention to multifarious details which were to attend the duties of one of the greatest leaders of all time. In this connection, it should be remembered that many of the greatest reformers of the Church throughout the ages have in this sense apparently benefited greatly from the 'wisdom of the Egyptians'. Paul, Augustine, Wycliffe, Luther, Calvin, Wesley, John Darby, Jonathan Edwards and John Sung, to name just a representative few, obviously found their sustained classical studies did not add one whit to revelation, but did help them preserve the integrity of the faith against sciences, falsely so-called, enabling them to transmit more effectively its unchanging message into the changing vocabulary of succeeding generations. We are commanded to love God with all our minds, but we have seen the tragic effect of a knowledge of the sciences being looked upon as something totally of this world and therefore suspect as a Christian vocation.

Young Christians, though possessing the capacity for

academic study, have been pressurised into leaving a university course unfinished in order to enter Bible college to prepare for the ministry. Unless, like Spurgeon, they have by nature an insatiable questing mind and a built-in capacity for analytical and synthetical study, they will find themselves hoping increasingly that the Lord has some prophetic word available every time 'Balaam's ass' opens his mouth! The 'wisdom of the Egyptians', at the very least, has the value of preparing a voice for God that would be intelligible in the courts of the Pharaohs.

The discipline of a felt destiny
That Moses felt the tug towards the leadership of his nation before he knew the essential nature of his call is evident. In Hebrews, we are told that when he had come of age, he refused to be called the son of Pharaoh's daughter and chose instead to share in affliction with the people of God (Heb. 11:24, 25). Then Stephen says explicitly that when he had come to full forty years of age, he took it into his heart to visit his people Israel and, unknowingly, then reached the point of no return (Acts 7:23–9; cf. Exod. 2:11ff.). Now, these two decisions were not necessarily simultaneous. To come of age in Jewry meant to be twelve years old. It is an interesting conjecture, therefore, that this young Jew, though surrounded by the luxury of court life and the indulgence of his Egyptian foster-mother, and in his teens when ideals are often crystallised and things are seen in black and white perspective, may have begun to make his allegiance to his own people vocal without thought to the consequences. Perhaps the resourceful Miriam had continued to influence her brother?

The Bible is silent on many of these things, but we can infer from a comparison of Stephen's remarks and the records of tradition[1] that the mighty deeds and words that took Moses on a successful military expedition against the Ethiopians may have been a well-meant attempt by Pharaoh to cool this rising Jewish ardour. Possibly at some time Moses had thought somehow to use his influence at court to turn the clock back on the Pharaohs and become another Joseph, to better the conditions of his enslaved people. But God was not interested in a more pampered people in an idolatrous environment, but in a free people back on what proved to be a long and tortuous road to monotheism.

Indeed, we now see from the subsequent sad history of Moses's entire generation that Egyptian idolatry had profoundly influenced their attitude towards God and a consistent worship of Him. They desperately needed rather costly grandstand seats, while Egypt's many gods were made to look utterly ludicrous before a man with a mere shepherd's rod to represent the unseen and forgotten Yahweh. Four hundred years of physical slavery was the very least of Israel's problems!

The discipline of renounced security
Moses in a Pharaoh's court was God's man for another reason. Israel's future leader needed to be a man who knowingly turned his back once and for all on the riches and security of court life and could therefore later stand before his jealous accusers as having been impervious to bribery, partiality or covetousness among his own people. It is doubtful if a slave-led revolt would have produced leadership of this quality.

Give me a missionary who has gone through the crucible of renunciation to get to the field and I will feel happier about his staying power. The principal of an Australasian missionary institute tells of a student who had been offered a new car to stay at home; another, full fees at some other type of training where the emphasis is definitely not missionary; another, a one-third increase in salary to remain with the firm; another, company training up to commercial jet-captain level if he stayed; and another faced the threat of losing a farm that his parents had bought specially for him. One candidate was even threatened with court action to restrain him. As potential missionary leaders, they will all be better for the tests.

The discipline of defeat
Moses also suffered the discipline of defeat, but we can see that defeat, with God, does not mean ultimate disaster. He can turn our early failures into our deepest lessons to profit. From one point of view, Moses's capacity for righteous indignation, which could break a cruel Egyptian's pate as well as the hewn stone of Sinai's despised commandments, was all part of the greatness of the man. A leader's personal capacity for moral leadership will depend upon his capacity to feel deeply enough. But the sand will not long bury the effects of unwise zeal!

A missionary in Japan is reputed to have tied a rope round a wayside shrine, hitching it to his jeep and then towing it through the town in triumph, no doubt feeling that he had dealt a killing blow at deeply-entrenched idolatry! The ensuing stench of such a 'dead Egyptian in the sand' would not be easily removed, even if the missionary himself left to learn elsewhere both the language of the people and the secrets of more spiritual warfare.

Moses's impetuous efforts to better the lot of his people precipitated forty years' isolation in the desert as a shepherd (Acts 7:29f.), but what better training could a future leader of Israel have than to care for animals so renowned for their stupidity and so utterly dependent upon their shepherd? Further, if again and again he would have to stand with nerve and integrity unshattered by a multitude calling for his blood and blaming him personally for every necessary chastening that came their way, he needed the discipline of waiting for God's purposes to ripen, the kind of aloneness with God that puts 'eras in their brains'. A. W. Tozer once suggested that Enoch must have been lonely, and Noah too: 'The weakness of so many modern Christians is that they feel too much at home in the world—they have lost their pilgrim character. They aren't lonely; but neither are they saints.'

Joseph did not only suffer from an unjust imprisonment; later the hope of possible release was denied him. But the extra two years' imprisonment had their purpose. The 'collar of iron' (cf. Ps. 105:18) may not have been long on his neck, but the iron entered his very soul. God seems to have no 'instant' leaders. It took eighty years' preparation to get forty years' service out of Moses.

From despair to the discipline of hesitant obedience
The next important element in Moses's call centres round his encounter with God in the desert (Exod. 3:2–4:17). The despair that follows defeat, and which with many of us is little more than injured pride, now gives place to true humility, and the Lord seems to meet Moses on his own terms.

The pendulum has swung from the 'I will' of mistaken zeal, to the 'I cannot' of utter despair. Then it settles into the modified refusal of 'I will not; send another', finally stopping at the 'I will, but . . .', and Aaron enters to make it a whittled call and a shared responsibility that proves his brother to be a broken reed. It is interesting to see how God used signs to keep Moses aware of his nothingness, but at the same time the very same signs became the insignia of his office and the assurance of unlimited resources.

Even a desert shrub could feel the heat of God's holy presence without being consumed; neither its character nor its shape was changed. So it is with God's dealings with men. According to Paul, God puts His treasure in earthern vessels so that the excellence of the power may be of Him and not of us. The bush remained bush. The vessel remains vessel, a mere common earthenware jar, so that by contrast the presence of the transforming power of God cannot be denied. It is amazing what God has been able to do with men who have refused to touch the glory. At a South American conference of missionaries and nationals, the foreigners asked the national pastors which qualities they wanted in missionaries to their field. One replied that they did not want missionaries who believed themselves to be fourth members of the Holy Trinity.

Moses remained, as it were, just desert scrub. The symbol of his office remained just a shepherd's rod, the hand that grasped it leprous with the memory of foolish zeal when he plucked it from his bosom, and yet that very hand, under command, could now grasp the rod turned serpent—by its tail, mind you! A whole nation would shudder and eventually yield its slaves. Seas were to fall apart and rocks yield sweet water at the raising of the rod.

God remained, thankfully to Moses, the God of the bush. But those flames, which to the end meant the presence of One whose very love was holiness on fire, licked into the remotest corners of Egyptian idolatry, scourged the pilgrim camp of its rebels, and finally, yes, burnt even Moses, right where his meekness ought to have been. God cannot tolerate human petulance as a poor imitation of His own holy wrath, and punishes His servant because a general's mistake is so very much more far-reaching than that of a private.

The cost of disciplining others
The call of Moses, therefore, was tested to the last and the cost was cumulative. The bitterest element of this cost was no doubt the constant misrepresentation on the part of those he was trying to help. This seems to be a common experience with true leaders. Edmund Burke once admonished public servants saying, 'Those who would carry on the great public schemes must be proof against the most fatiguing delays, the most mortifying

disappointments, the most shocking insults, and worst of all, the most presumptuous judgments of the ignorant upon their designs.' Moses tasted this bitter cup to the full.

In that felt darkness, just before the dawn of deliverance, the harassed Israelites naturally blamed Moses for their increased burdens. Actually, if the whip of extra pressure had not been applied to their backs in Egypt, it is debatable whether they would have been willing to leave their fleshpots, the onions and garlic, to follow Moses to freedom. Then, when the water was found bitter at Marah, when they experienced hunger in the Desert of Sin and thirst at Rephidim (Exod. 15:23–17:7), Moses was to blame. That Korah and his friends should plot a *coup d'état* out of envy for his office was hard enough to take, but what must it have meant to have Aaron and Miriam turn against him over his foreign wife (cf. Num. 16 and 12)? If it was because she happened to be a coloured woman, then Miriam suffered in judgment from something a good deal more distinctive than the mere pigment of the skin!

It is a measure of his greatness that, on every such occasion but one, Moses would not negate his call. He refused to head up another race as a heaven-sent alternative and threw himself upon the Lord who called him, to vindicate, praying for the people as his very own, though they would do all they could to disown him.

Moses therefore can give us a robust Christian answer to the criticism that will inevitably dog a leader's footsteps and that is at times the portion of every Christian. We have again and again seen the Lord Himself vindicate hard-pressed, unfairly-treated servants of God, and when the Lord does it fewest are hurt, and the least needs to be said. In Moses we see written large the cost of being a kind of public conscience to his generation. He was called to be angry at sin, very angry indeed if he were only to reflect God's holy wrath; at sin, certainly, but he was not to sin himself.

Finally, I believe we can see in Moses something of the cost of really being identified with the people to whom the Lord sends us. Moses rises to his greatest heights when pleading for his people in Exodus 32. Nowhere does he come closer to the One who finally was to offer His very body as an intercessory bridge of reconciliation between an angry God and a sinning people. For this alone, Moses could well have earned Scripture's supreme accolade in Deuteronomy 18:15, 'The Lord your God will raise up for you a prophet *like me* from among you, from your brethren.'

1. See Josephus, *Antiquities*, ii. 10.

3

The Call of Gideon

After Moses and Joshua, the record of Israel's pilgrimage is a sorry one, to say the least. On the one hand, Judges reveals how dependent the masses were upon convinced and dedicated leadership. Their faithfulness to Yahweh seemed to depend utterly upon the faithfulness of their leaders, though with no Bible in every man's hand it was little wonder that the spiritual temperature rose and fell according to the spiritual and moral heat of the leader in vogue. Usually there seems to have been a time-lag, and periods of depravity left the masses so anaemic that there was hardly ever a full-blooded response to subsequent drastic and needed change. On the other hand, God chose to deliver the people from servitude in ways that suited the times in which they lived, and by men who had very little of which to boast.

The inconspicuous origin
Othoniel no doubt could say that he was the son of the younger brother of Caleb, but that is stretching it a bit thin. Ehud was left-handed, Shamagar slaughtered hundreds with an ox-goad, Deborah was a 'mere woman' and in her regime Sisera did not fall to Barak's prowess, but to a woman's ingenuity. And as for the fifth judge, Gideon, he came of a poor, obscure family of the smal-

34

lest tribe. The call of God to leadership of necessity comes to a man when he is least conscious that he deserves the privilege.

Gideon's family were idolaters. Gideon himself, 'one who cuts down', i.e. a warrior, when his call came was threshing out wheat with a mere stick away from the normal threshing-floor to avoid detection by the ravaging Midianites (Judg. 6 : 1–12). The devastation had continued for seven years, with the occupying nomads like a plague of locusts devouring all before them. God's people, instead of enjoying to the full the fruit of the land for which their forebears had fought 200 years before, were now peering out upon their once-conquered foe from caves and dens in the mountains. Humiliation is not the least effective of God's instruments in bringing a people to an end of themselves.

God's declared purpose
Gideon naturally was surprised at the angel's salutation (6 : 12). It was some name to live up to, even if he was supposed to be a warrior. But 'you mighty man of valour' must have been a prophecy of what God intended to make him, and least of all an attempt to sting him into living up to the name he already had.

When Simon received his 'Peter' he was obviously a long way from living up to it, even if he did have a flash of spiritual insight as to the Person of Christ. Jesus could say 'So send I you' to the disciples when they had no intention of going anywhere, and out of fear had the door locked besides—from the inside! Paul calls the Corinthian Christians 'saints' when they were riotously belying that very appellation, but Paul obviously was convinced that even in Corinth they *could be* saints—otherwise he had no true gospel.

The place of no return
The call to leadership involves clear-cut goals with unwavering initiative. Gideon's destruction of the altar to

Baal and the nearby Asherah grove (Judg. 6:25–32) has, with local modifications, been repeated again and again on idolatrous mission fields. Japanese have been known to burn their household idols at one hearing of the gospel, but this has not always been the case. One lady we know did not for some time get rid of the eight family gods she had worshipped, even though they were now meaningless to her. Ancestral worship can weave heavy threads of obligation and sentiment not easily broken.

But Gideon, on that fateful night, despite his fears, must have realised that the morning light would bring swift reaction to his flinging a glove in the face of the whole vested interest of the Baal system. The biblical record implies just a simple, though hesitant, act of obedience and we wonder to what extent Gideon shared God's holy wrath at the real cause of Israel's humiliation. No link is made between the faithful rebuke of the unknown prophet of Judges 6:7–10 and the call of Gideon in verses 11–16 of the same chapter, but he was in no condition to lead an idolatrous people back to God without an uncompromising stand in his own home. In leadership, 'only a passionate purity is safe'. Only an open declaration on God's side will awaken the sleeping conscience of some who have backslidden.

How often have we seen this! Nothing so convinces either a backslidden believer or a bewildered unbeliever as to the reality of a person's experience of God than to see him wholly sold out to obedience, cost what it may. I recall the story told me one day about a Japanese medical student who became a Christian in his third year and who soon felt convinced that he should be in the ministry. He thereupon wrote to his father to tell him that he was leaving his course to go into a theological seminary. The father wrote back and, in typical Oriental fashion, applied the strongest pressure he knew to prevent him doing any such thing. He would take his life rather than see his son so disgrace himself and his family.

The son sent him a telegram with the one word '*Shine*' ('Die!'). I held my breath when listening to the narrative for Japanese will take their lives for less than that, but apparently the father still lives and the son is in the ministry. The strength of the son's purpose and conviction made opposition fruitless.

Certainly the zeal with which the first and later the continuing initiative is taken is a vital secret in successful leadership. Gideon, perhaps unwittingly, had cut the painter so cleanly that he could not go back. True, the initial break with the sorry past had seemed timorous enough and he hardly dared move without some spectacular sign to confirm the next command (Judg. 6:36–40), but it surely is not without significance that he was only taken possession of by the Spirit (verse 34) to utter a challenge to the whole nation after these initial steps of obedience. Perhaps his continuing hesitance made it necessary for the Spirit to 'clothe Himself with Gideon', for it is a singular expression for the measure in which Gideon experienced the Spirit's enabling.

The response to decisive leadership
The response was overwhelming. The nation longed for leadership. We all do. Even if the goal be far off and difficult, its realisation is never questioned if we are given leadership we can trust. Only let not the leader be as is pictured so tellingly by A. W. Tozer, 'trying to discover the direction the people want him to lead them, and then scrambling ahead of them trying to look like Moses on his way out of Egypt'. 'Such a leader', he wrote in an editorial in *The Alliance Witness*, 'will send up a trial balloon and then boldly set out in the direction of the wind, doing his best to create the impression that the wind consulted him before it began to blow.' Dwight Eisenhower illustrated this positively from another angle at a conference of his war staff. He took a piece of string when they were discussing the subject of leadership, and laid it on his desk saying, 'Look, if I try to push

it I don't get anywhere. But if I pull it I can take it anywhere I want.'

The initiative maintained
The important thing for Gideon, then, was to retain the
thrust of initiative. It was not enough to declare himself
wholly on the side of Yahweh and in open warfare
against Baal; he must now attack the fruit of Israel's
compromise in the enemy around them. The trumpet
summoned five tribes to warfare.

Viscount Montgomery's tactics in the African desert
serve to illustrate the same point. He demanded 100
per cent belief in ultimate victory, whereas his predeces-
sor had been making plans for defeat. Montgomery deliberately destroyed his bases and brought everything
into the battle front, making no provision for defeat.
He ruthlessly eliminated the unfit. He himself abandoned the comforts of an established headquarters,
took to a caravan and deliberately associated himself
with the troops in a psychological attack first of all on
the prevailing low morale. Incidentally, could anything
have been lower than the morale of Israel in the days
of the Judges?

The will to win, coupled with deliberately planned
attacks, always keeping the initiative from the enemy,
laid the foundations for ultimate victory in Africa. Can
the same thing not be said in respect to victory in the
Christian life, and that of the leader in particular? Defeat must not even be contemplated. 'Sin shall not have
dominion', said Paul (Rom. 6:14, A.V.). Like the para-
lytic whom Jesus healed, we are commanded to take up
our bed, because we will not be needing it again—certainly not to beg from! The best defence is attack, and
the leader will find that he must take the initiative in
policy-making, and in definite plans of outright confrontation with entrenched evil, both in the world
around him and within him. Perhaps the enemy within
is the most elusive, and we find the flesh capable of the

most extraordinary versatility in hiding its identity. Admiral Nelson believed that the best defence of Britain lay outside the enemy's own ports and challenged his captains saying, 'I rely on you, that I do not miss the enemy.'

In the world of the church at large, the same thing holds. A. W. Tozer reckoned that the power of God always hovers over the frontiers. 'Miracles have accompanied our advances and have ceased when and where we have allowed ourselves to become satisfied and ceased to advance.'[1]

Divine mathematics

Gideon's advances were conditioned on the one hand by his determination to have some further indubitable sign that he was on the path of victory and, on the other, by God's determination to make it abundantly clear both to Gideon and to Israel at large that the coming victory was going to be just as miraculous as the sign.

Alexander MacLaren pungently suggests that after the careful choice of the 300 in Judges 7:4–8, Gideon had fewer persons but not fewer men. Whatever the precise significance was, Gideon's irreducible minimum is a healthy corrective for the Christian worker who gives way to the thought that God is on the side of the big battalions and 'we must get together or perish'. So often on the mission field there are not enough hands to go around but young Christians *will* persist in leaving for the city as soon as they graduate from college. 'Leaving us,' says the rural missionary, 'back where we started.' But when the Spirit of God really clothes Himself with a dedicated national, though the numbers be small, sometimes more can be accomplished in a few weeks than the missionary can accomplish in years.

From our limited experience it can also be said that God's answers to our prayers along these lines have come in such a way that it has been evident that He alone has done it. The Gideons have not always been of our choosing! Samuel could see a king in Eliab. Our part in great measure is to have the privilege of praying for that which the Lord wants to do, even if our Gideon surprises us. Gideon for his part will also need his encouragements, though not every leader will have the privilege of a listening ear to the panic-filled conversation of his enemies (Judg. 7:9–15).

In these days, victory in any given situation is not always preceded by such heavenly assurances. Potentially, victory *is* already ours, but to see it realised in the hearts of others calls for battle 'till the other fellow cracks', as Montgomery would have said. For it is much more important to fight well when things are going badly than when things are going well.

Reaction to victory
Gideon met his first major setback in the Ephraimite reaction to the Midianite victory (Judg. 8:1–3). Their jealous reaction to the conduct of the war was childish in the extreme and Gideon's soft reply was couched in terms that suited their psychological age. Ephraim never did grow up. The leader may be tempted to think the same of fellow-workers on occasion. 'Most people,' as Fowler Hamilton has well said, 'are down on things they are not up on', and even victory has to be handled in a way that spreads the credit thin.

Often it requires the verdict of time to discover whether or not a person's leadership has been successful; meanwhile the majority meet each unpopular measure with vituperation. John F. Kennedy, in his book *Profiles in Courage*,[2] left a fascinating account of leaders in American history who were willing to go against public opinion for the sake of the larger good of the nation. Men like Thomas Hart Benton could 'despise the bubble popularity', and those like Edmund G. Ross could stand alone against enormous odds, looking down, as he said, 'into my own grave'. Men of tender scruple and far-reaching principle in public affairs have sometimes been prematurely buried from excess of grief. Certainly they have on many occasions been dismissed as political figures until subsequent history has fully but belatedly vindicated their foresight.

Amy Carmichael in her book *Kohila* puts it in words that will find a ready response in the hearts of many a leader today:

> Zeal to promote the common good, whether it be by devising anything ourselves, or revising that which hath been laboured by others, deserveth certainly much respect and esteem, but yet findeth but cold entertainment in the world. It is welcomed with suspicion instead of love, and with emulation instead of thanks, and if there be any hole left for cavil to enter (and cavil, if it does not find a hole, will make one), it is sure to be misconstrued, and in danger to be condemned. . . .[3]

In Gideon's case, the Ephraimites were doubtless motivated in their cavil by fear of any material loss in the spoils of victory, seeing theirs was a belated entry into the conflict. Today, jealousy of the same kind more often arises from envy at another leader's success rather than any desire for material gain. King Saul suffered from this horrid spiritual jaundice to the full. The Jews finally murdered Jesus because of it. The leader will need to guard his spirit from bitterness and if necessary let the God of history vindicate him and his motives in a way that will do most good to the cavillers and to later students of history.

Finally, a note on the dangers of successful leadership. Gideon quite naturally rode on a high crest of exuberant appreciation and, while refusing the proffered kingship of the nation on the one hand, he gave in to an impulse on an issue that was both indicative of his lack of discernment and of the extent of his own influence (Judg. 8:22–27).

Some feel that Gideon's desire for an ephod was a harmless personal affair with no thought of any conflict with Shiloh, but he reckoned without the determination of the masses to associate their deliverance with Gideon himself rather than Yahweh, and with his ways of worship as a religious rallying centre. The slightest whim or indulgence of a leader of such nation-wide esteem can have profound consequences.

The consequences of moral lethargy in leaders
Gideon had in fact a glorious opportunity to lead his people back to Yahweh and encourage in the nation at large what he had been able to do in his own family, but his personal ephod, his self-centred religion in Ophrah, stole his thunder. He could produce children by the score, but upon his death the way his seventy sons were all destroyed by Abimelech was to indicate how pampered they had been. There seems to have been little or no effort to lead either them or the children of Israel in a disciplined Yahweh-centred life. Upon his own death 'the people of Israel turned again and played the harlot after the Baals . . .' (8:33).

In different language the same sad story is written large in Christian circles today. Young converts naturally feel attached to their spiritual father. Their whole religious experience becomes centred in his personality, but they fail to catch the significance of his convictions or themselves drink from the source of his inspiration. Certain cultures on the mission field also lend themselves to this very danger. The missionary deputises for his converts without realising it. He may be undiscerning enough to revel in the warmth of the love and appreciation of the national converts without taking steps to see to their spiritual independence from him. When he leaves, the work collapses.

Or, on the home front, the outstanding Evangelical is strangely succeeded by a ministry that may be scholarly enough and decorated with no little pulpit eloquence, yet the elders or deacons are not sufficiently discerning to see through his lip-service to the evangelical cause. Indeed, church officers have been known to welcome a drastic change in emphasis to the extent that the cutting edge of the church in that district is completely gone. Surely, therefore, a sure test of the worth of a man's ministry is the measure in which he produces other leaders who are not dependent upon the inspiration of his immediate presence and who have personal convictions that are biblical to the extent of being costly to keep.

After the overthrow of Midian, Israel enjoyed peace for the whole of the subsequent forty years of Gideon's office (Judg. 8–28). Howard Morgan once remarked that 'the man most sought after as a public servant combines the best qualities of the milkman's horse: he must raise no important problems and he must know where to stop.' It would appear that Gideon kept the peace by blinking at Baal and stopped taking the moral and spiritual initiative at the very time when Israel was ripe for reform. May the Lord keep us from being content without holy contention and evading problems for the sake of a peaceful life!

1. A. W. Tozer, *Paths to Power* (Marshall, Morgan and Scott).
2. Published by Harper Brothers.
3. Amy W. Carmichael, *Kohila* (S.P.C.K.), p. 24.

4

The Call of Timothy

Timothy was no apostle, to dismay us with an impressive array of supernatural gifts. True, he worked with apostles. He was probably converted through Paul's ministry and was certainly called into the closest fellowship with that prince of all missionary leaders, but he belongs to the post-apostolic age—at least, to the end of the age of the initial Twelve—and therefore in a special sense he belongs to us.

Timothy's background
He belongs to us, too, because he came from a divided home, as is the experience of many a Christian leader today. We learn from Acts 16:1 that his father was a Greek while his mother was a Jewish Christian; 2 Timothy 1:5 tells us of the faith of both his grandmother and his mother. The lack of reference to Timothy's father—even if he had died in his son's childhood—and the fact that Timothy had not been circumcised at birth, lead one to deduce that his father was a Gentile.

How his mother Eunice could have been persuaded into marriage with a Gentile Greek when she had a devout believing mother herself is difficult to understand. Alexander Whyte heavily labours this point, feeling that

44

there must have been a serious departure from the Jewish faith,[1] but F. F. Bruce in his commentary on Acts suggests that the Jews of Asia were less exclusive than those of Palestine in their relations with the Gentile world.[2]

Be that as it may, it looks as though the spiritual side of Timothy's life came from his mother and grandmother alone. There was not even a Jewish proselyte father to encourage him. We can only guess at the overwhelming joy of the two women at having Timothy follow so closely where they perhaps had, at a crucial time of testing, followed afar off. They were to prove abundantly that God does not break the bruised reed nor quench the smoking wick.

In this connection I am reminded of Solomon. He was the second son of Bathsheba, the woman who of all David's wives one would have thought least probable to be the queen mother. But Solomon, 'beloved by his God', was not to be frustrated in his personal destiny by the shame of his mother. Indeed, 2 Samuel 7:12, 13 would lead us to think that Solomon was promised as king even before David fell ready victim to Bathsheba's attractiveness and the resulting cumulative effects of escaping from his own folly.

In the Matthew account of our Lord's ancestors, it is interesting to note that Bathsheba is in the list ('the wife of Uriah', Matt. 1:6). Not only so, but the only two other women mentioned are Tamar, who produced Perez as one of the set of twins by her own father-in-law Judah, and Rahab, presumably the harlot, who gave birth to Boaz. To have come from a long line of devoted servants of God is a great privilege. Some of the Lord's servants very obviously have inherited some sweet graces and a steady depth of character in this way, but it is not the only school where God produces His chosen servants.

More often than not we can point to the mother as the most important and influential element in a child's character training, as was clearly the case with Timothy. Perhaps he owed his rather timorous disposition to the strong influence of the two women, specially if we can presume that his father died when he was young, but if they sensed he had an overweening confidence in their opinions, they did the very best thing in soaking his receptive mind with the Word of God. Happily enough, they lived in an age when it was not thought wrong to encourage the memorisation of the Word of God 'before he could make up his own mind'.

Timothy's call
Timothy's call to full-time service came as a personal challenge through Paul the apostle, who presumably had led him to the Saviour (1 Tim. 1:2). In Timothy's day, the massive, multi-phased missionary propaganda machine and organisational diversity of the present time, with all their information for the would-be missionary, did not exist. Today, the challenge to foreign or home service may come to us in a very impersonal way: through hearing a radio message, through the reading of a missionary biography, or listening to the testimony of a number of missionaries at one meeting whose experiences both bewilder and attract us, but who are themselves perhaps too far removed from our status in life to make personal conversation desirable. A missionary convention can catch us up in a rising swell of public opinion and concern, but a decision to be a missionary often follows later upon cold reflection. It comes from a sense of call that is increasingly inescapable.

With Timothy, however, the call was simplicity itself. Acts 16:3 records that 'Paul wanted Timothy to accompany him', and that was that! We can only imagine whether it was a challenge from which Timothy shrank or whether he had secretly longed for the great privilege of joining the apostle in his mission, but when the call did come it was simply a matter of following the leadership and challenge of another life.

Paul's calling him to himself decided Timothy's vocation.

Nor is this singular. I recall reading of a great meeting in England when an aged veteran of the dawn of modern missions challenged the students of the theological college of his day with the unmet needs of the African continent and only got a positive response when, in his final peroration, he touched their consciences at the thought of a dying man now determined to return to Africa because they were obviously reluctant to go!

J. C. Pollock in his book *A Cambridge Movement*[3] tells of a conversation between Stanley Smith, one of the Cambridge Seven, and William Cassells. Afterwards Smith wrote, 'Had an interesting talk with Cassells, he is much interested in China. May the Lord send him out with me.' Actually Cassells had been thinking of going to Africa with the Church Missionary Society, but now decided 'he should be beside Smith in China'.

Montague Beauchamp, another of the famous Cambridge Seven, also owed much to personal conversation and challenge, this time from Stanley Smith and C. T. Studd. These men influenced their whole generation because of who they were. J. C. Farthing once said, 'When men whom everybody had heard of and many had known personally, came up and said "I am going out myself", we were brought individually face to face with the heathen abroad.'

It was the personal challenge, therefore, of another life—an utterly dedicated life—rather than the distant needs of the heathen that changed the course of affairs for them and led them to a similar dedication and life-purpose. The principle is soundly biblical. Paul without hesitation could challenge believers to follow him, even as he sought to follow the Saviour. A. B. Simpson once pointed out that 'not many rivers run into the sea. Most rivers run into other rivers. Similarly, the best

missionaries are followers and helpers, emptying streams
of blessing into others. No man can be a trusted leader
until he has first become a broken and obedient fol-
lower.' This, then, was the essence of Timothy's initial call and his faithfulness in that path that led to an
ever wider ministry and growing personal responsibility
as a leader of others.

Timothy's training
   a. Working together. In one sense, Timothy's training
began before Paul had actually laid a challenging hand
upon his shoulder. In Acts 14, Luke records the dramatic
turn of events that left Paul apparently dead after the
stoning among a group of fanatical Jews in Lystra—
Timothy's home city. If Timothy did not see the incident with his own eyes, he would soon hear all about it,
and possibly at the same time have seen the ugly evidence of the brutal assault on his future leader's body.
When Paul called him to follow, therefore, there would
be no hankering after the romance of missions! Mark
had already had enough and turned back (Acts 15:38)
but, to Timothy's credit, the possible cost of having such
an adventurous companion and leader did not deter
him from a life-sized affirmation to Paul's call in his
subsequent visit to Timothy's city (Acts 16:3).
   If the unconscious training of Paul's example had prepared him to accept the challenge without misconcep-
tion, he was soon to meet in full consciousness the effect
of obedience as they set out for Europe together, though
it was Paul and Silas who suffered the beating in the
Philippian jail.
   Modern missionary training might well take a long,
hard look at the way Paul trained future Church leaders.
He had no need later to write to a discouraged Timothy
in Ephesus saying, 'Now, Timothy, surely you will recall my lectures on pastoral theology. You would do
well to look them over again: after all they were nicely

cyclostyled for this very reason and you will find some very useful hints on how to deal with fellows like Alexander, and the kind of stuff to look for in prospective elders!'

No, Paul could appeal from the vantage-point of having taken a lion's share of suffering in front of Timothy, and he now expected him to bear his share with fortitude (2 Tim. 1 : 8; 3 : 10–12). He could urge him to follow the pattern of sound words that Timothy had heard from Paul's own lips in the confrontation of meetings in synagogues and the journeys throughout Asia Minor together (2 Tim. 1 : 13). They laboured, journeyed, taught, ate, slept and suffered together.

Detmar Scheunemann, who is engaged in Bible school work in Indonesia, has some pertinent things to say along the same lines about the training of young nationals for missionary work. In an address given to foreign and national missionary leaders in 1968, he said :

> Every year, teams are going out from here, and that really means training. We don't believe that training can only be done here and that what they receive in the classroom is enough. Many lessons are learned on the wayside as we face the powers of darkness and many other difficulties of everyday life. The teachers are together with the students. Do the teachers sleep together with students or not? We went on a ship together; it happened that some of the crew were giving their cabins to us as teachers. This can be a real temptation. I always slept under heaven on deck together with the team.
>
> You have to get used to these situations. These are small matters but have great meaning when it comes to training. Sometimes the Lord asks for sacrifice. We were to go out with teams and were asking the Lord to lead us, though in my heart I

wanted to go to Timor. I had been there before and the Lord had really worked there after our visit so I longed to go back. But the Lord said, 'No, you must go to West Java.' In the spiritual sense that was a barren area. I was to go with a mixed team. This meant that I could not go alone; I could only go with my wife. But if my wife came then the children had to come too. It meant several weeks away and the children could not be left behind. However, it seemed that my wife could not go for she had for four years poured out her strength in the service of the gospel. But we faced the challenge of God's Word. Israel faced the challenge of an open door into the promised land, but because of lack of faith they did not enter. The result was that later when they did want to enter they were not permitted. They wept and wandered in the wilderness. So, the Lord spoke to us as a family, 'The door is open— go!' The Lord gave us the necessary courage to take the children and it was wonderful.

Although we were travelling several weeks, and those who know Indonesia know what that means, the Lord was going before and preparing a place for the children. . . . At that time, we did not know that we were training families, though we had a married couple in the team, but some of the lessons they received then they could never have received in the school through our service together as a couple. It is when we work together in teams that we are tested and weaknesses are revealed. You have to live together to prove there are no differences between nationalities and colours of skin.

The stories of some of these teams reads like the New Testament all over again. Such training is costly for the tutors in particular, but where can you produce an apostolic ministry without apostolic cost? Not least, it calls for total commitment to life with the candidates themselves.

b. Adaptability. Timothy obviously learnt much from being with the apostle, but he also had to adapt himself readily to the demands of that discipleship in terms of availability, and in terms of bodily discomfort, for Paul demanded that he be circumcised so as not to offend the legal scruples of the Jews to whom he would so often minister in the future (Acts 16:3).

Thus to regularise Timothy's status in Jewish eyes apparently presented no problem of consistency with Paul who, in writing to the Galatians, insisted that Gentiles should not be circumcised (Gal. 5:2, 3). In one sense, Timothy was both Jew and Gentile, yet he was neither. Certainly now that he was emancipated in Christ he would be even more indifferent to the claims of the legalisers among the Jews, but he was apparently willing enough to undergo some minor surgery if it would make him more acceptable to the Jews for the gospel's sake. They certainly would not be able to argue that he had only become a Christian because he had no desire to be a Jew!

On the mission field, this kind of willingness to conform to local custom for the sake of the gospel can involve a major adjustment and a profound culture shock. For some missionaries, it is enough that they have been asked to modify their dress styles, perhaps involving a reversion to modes long abandoned at home. It may be a matter of dying to well-developed taste-buds in a life that till then has known nothing but the indulgence of every personal whim. It may be just a simple matter of adjustment to a completely new courtesy code that is neutral in itself, but to disregard it or baulk at it is just very poor taste. 'Why should I change? It was good enough for me at home, why not now? Let others adjust for a change. Besides, it's plain silly', is the unspoken or very outspoken reaction to situations that are just too baffling for the Western extrovert. So, insignificant but very revealing breaches of etiquette continue to raise the eyebrows of every cultured visitor. Certainly, to try to present the gospel without an honest effort to maintain the honorifics in the language is to render objectionable the very message we have come to proclaim.

Admittedly, today one often wonders who it is who suffers most from culture shock. A stiff-necked, self-centred missionary certainly will, but what of the national's own reaction to the foreigner who has just come out of a church situation in certain parts of the West where modes of thought and dress are 'way out'?

Of course, in some cultures there are areas where to conform would be to compromise. Foreigners are guilty of participating in heathen religious rites just to be pleasant and obliging and in so doing convey an impression of connivance that they far from feel. On the other hand, a few are over-scrupulous and see idolatry where there is none, and read into some seasonal customs and festivals a religious significance that has long been lost to the nationals themselves. One missionary is known to have refused to use stamps on which there is the facial image of a bygone emperor who was once an object of worship. I can imagine that Paul would have sat very lightly to that kind of sensitiveness.

Some may argue that if Paul in his willingness to be all things to all men had not joined the Jewish group under a vow and shaved his head (the second recorded time, incidentally) with them to show his continuing reverence for the law (Acts 21:17–31), his ministry might not have been so violently cut short. No one can say what would have happened at that tense festival, however, even if Paul had not agreed to a public display of obedience to his country's customs. The effect could well have been just the same; indeed, one of the main reasons he was mobbed was not because of the shared

vow but because of his open fellowship with an Ephes-
ian believer and the false rumours that resulted (Acts
21:29). Paul was only being consistent with his stated
principles in 1 Corinthians 9:19–23 and 10:32, 33 when
he declared himself willing to be all things to all men and
give offence to none, so that as many as possible might
be led to the emancipation that is in Christ alone. To
him, circumcision was nothing and uncircumcision was
nothing (1 Cor. 7:19) but, as F. F. Bruce has said, 'a
truly emancipated spirit such as Paul's is not in bondage
to its own emancipation.'[4]

Timothy's commission
Finally, Timothy's call involved a commission to be
fulfilled. Three times in the two Pastoral Epistles to
Timothy, Paul makes reference to an ordination cere-
mony as a basis for differing appeals.

From 1 Timothy 1:18 and 4:14 it would appear that
there had been a prophetical indication that Timothy
was to be set aside for full-time service. No doubt it was
a conviction that Paul felt quite deeply before he called
Timothy to himself. Whether or not the elders who
prayed with Paul at the time also shared the same conviction is uncertain, though the gift of prophecy at that
time was no doubt a much clearer faculty and more
individualised than prophecy is thought of today.
But there was not only the gift recognised in Timothy
on that occasion; there was also a gift bestowed, for
in 2 Timothy 1:6 he is urged to rekindle the
gift that he had received at the time of laying on of
hands.

Paul, at two different turning-points in his own life,
had been prayed for in a similar way (Acts 9:17; 13:3),
and perhaps the deep significance of what transpired
on those occasions constrained him to appeal to this
crisis in Timothy's life also. Whatever the gift was that
he received on that occasion, it could be neglected on
the one hand (1 Tim. 4:14) or rekindled on the other

(2 Tim. 1:6). From a comparison of related passages one feels that if it were not a special experience of the filling of the Holy Spirit, it was certainly some kind of anointing with a view to the task that lay ahead.

In the case of those contemplating full-time service today, also, the gift already bestowed needs recognition. Before we set our eyes upon some distant field of service, or decide to serve the Lord in some capacity at home, we need to have an unshakable assurance that this is a calling that simply cannot be denied—an assurance deepened by the fact that godly men have perhaps recognised the gift before we even felt it and are not just giving into our whims so as not to discourage us.

I recall meeting a Salvation Army officer soon after my conversion, and though it was the first time we had met, he suddenly said to me, 'Some day you are going to be a great preacher.' Perhaps he had the gift of prophecy plus an addiction to exaggeration, but certainly at that time the thought of being any kind of preacher was the furthest thing from my mind. On the other hand, he could have been a true prophet, and if I had rekindled the gift as I should, or not neglected the gift as I have, perhaps I could have been the kind of preacher of which he spoke.

The point is, however, that the recognition of the gift is something that others perform for us. It should be most evident to spiritual men, therefore, that we do have the gift already or will have the requisite gifts in the future for the service they feel the Lord is calling us to. Certainly it should be a conviction that they have and we share, before we have theological training. Both in the ministry at home and on the mission field are to be found those who have been encouraged to take such a training by well-meaning but mistaken minister friends, and the result is a theological diploma with facility in theological verbiage but a power that is all too conspicuous by its absence.

Missionaries are often so anxious to get their young

Timothy into Bible college so that they will have a national to take over when they go on furlough, or because they like so-and-so (he's such a magnificent interpreter!) that they pay his way through a theological college or seminary, or Bible school, expecting that the years of exposure to biblical truth are going to make him the man of God they long to see take their place. He may be the type who shines while with the foreigner but does not have enough academic ability or money to get a decent university education, and so is only too willing to take advantage of some free tuition and the possibility of a paid job at the end—if this money is so easy to come by. The mission to which I belong has from the beginning refrained from any promise of support for those desirous of theological study, and we do not regret this rather severe measure to ensure the reality of their call.

From a positive point of view, the call and training of Akira Hatori, the well-known radio evangelist in Japan, is a case in point. For ten years or so Miss Burnett (founder of the Central Japan Pioneer Mission), who had led him to the Lord, continued to pray that the Lord would also lead him into full-time service, feeling sure that that was his calling. He had subsequently gone into secular teaching in Tokyo and not till sickness laid him low did he listen to the Lord's voice and go back to her for study. He did a pressure course in Greek with her before going off to Fuller Seminary, Miss Burnett using funds she had saved for her furlough in order to pay his fare. Other missionaries were against the training of nationals abroad but Miss Burnett seemed to have an uncanny knack for seeing beyond the traditional and the accepted to a wider ministry than was the custom at the time, and so it has proved to be.

We need more pastors and missionaries with the prophetic gift who could encourage the hidden Timothys and see the latent in what is not always patent. If we could see, in fact, the Peters in the Simons and the Pauls in Sauls, we would not be so short of those whom the pulpits really need.

1. Alexander Whyte, *Bible Characters (New Testament)* (Marshall, Morgan and Scott), p. 292.
2. F. F. Bruce, *The Book of Acts* (Marshall, Morgan and Scott), p. 322.
3. Published by John Murray. See also J. C. Pollock, *The Cambridge Seven* (Inter-Varsity Press).
4. F. F. Bruce, op. cit.

5

The Guided Life

The Christian maintains the right to lead others only if he himself is constantly being led by the Holy Spirit. In addition, he must know the basic principles common to all God's leading. For he must be able both to hear God's voice for himself and also to pass judgment on the so-called guidance of others, if called upon to do so, and in some cases even to find God's will for another life.

Guidance is first of all by the Word of God

a. This is a privilege that should not be abused by 'lucky dip' methods. God does and can guide His people by apparent chance selection of some Bible passage. Verses taken completely out of context have, on occasion, been God's voice to someone facing a special crisis. Guidance of such a nature is often for the yet immature and the great Shepherd of the sheep tenderly suits His leading to the spiritual capacities of the one being led. Spectacular incidents of such guidance, however, should not encourage a young Christian to take only occasional peeps at unrelated passages of the Bible instead of settling down to solid consecutive readings and study. He should not expect God always to guide in that way.

b. When a command from God is clear, it should never be circumvented by appeals to circumstances or to the inner voice of conviction, which, just by itself, can be most unreliable even in the more mature. Joshua was once commanded to stop praying (Josh. 7:10). He was seeking guidance in a time of national calamity. But there was no need to seek guidance—he already had it! Joshua 6:18 records the explicit command to be obeyed and then 7:15 records the penalty of any infringement. What remained was for Joshua to deal with evident sin in the camp.

To pray is not enough. Any path that would pander to our pride or rob us of fellowship with the Lord's children and take us from His highest for us calls not for prayer, but for instant rejection in the power of the Spirit. The Holy Spirit will never lead us to do something that is contrary to the Word of which He is the Author.

c. To use the name of Jesus in prayer does not take the place of the Word of God. The mere appending of the name of Jesus to prayer is no talisman or key to all that we want. 'Thou hast exalted thy word above all thy name,' the psalmist cries (Ps. 138:2 R.S.V. marg.).

In John 15:7 Jesus Himself reminds us that the measure in which the Word is abiding in us is an important condition to assurance in prayer. The name of Jesus and our acceptance in Him is the key to constant fellowship with the Father, but it is the Word that conveys His mind to us and guides us in paths that please him.

d. Guidance today is not, therefore, something apart from the Word. Old Testament and also New Testament saints, when lacking the written words, were often spoken to directly by the Spirit. How this happened is not explained in detail, but even today similar extraordinary visitations of the Spirit are not non-existent. A person's name has been known to be called as a check in time of grave danger, or some vision may also serve to arrest both sinner and saint alike. But this appears to be the exception rather than the rule. With singular force, a verse of the Bible will be recalled at some crucial time and, without doubt, this is a work of the Spirit and the more customary method of modern guidance in times of crisis.

Generally speaking, the Bible is our means of guidance in two different ways. First, by constant, faithful reading the Word gradually permeates our heart and conscience till we begin to think God's thoughts after Him. Our moral judgments and opinions become moulded till we are unconsciously guided in the multitude of moral choices in each day by the Word. In this connection, the words of Andrew Murray are much to the point: 'Little of the Word with little prayer is death to the spiritual life. Much of the Word with little prayer gives a sickly life. Much prayer with little of the Word gives more life but with little steadfastness. A full measure of the Word and prayer each day gives a healthy and powerful life.'

Secondly, in times of very special decision such as marriage, the choice of a life's work, and so on, it is wise to look to the Lord for some confirmation from the Word. I say confirmation rather than direction for, more often than not, the initial choice has to be made with little special conviction one way or another, nor with any definite circumstantial guidance. This is all part of the necessary tutelage in the school of discipline and faith and only when we have made the step of faith, with implicit confidence in the fact of His guiding, do we then find again and again the word of confirmation that 'this *is* the way—walk in it'.

Guidance is by the Spirit of God

   a. Guidance by the Spirit, promised to all who are born again by the Spirit (Rom. 8:14) is not apart from the Word. Even Christians can be subject to influence from various spirits and we are, therefore, commanded to try the spirits to see if they are of God or not (1 John 4:1). This should surely be in the light of the Word as is suggested in Hebrews 5:12–14.

It is not enough to 'feel guided'. It can be positively dangerous to wait, as it were, in the presence of God, and with a supposedly blank mind seek divine impressions. We leave ourselves open to all manner of evil influences, even if only to the dull spawning of human ingenuity.

The Holy Spirit never discards the Word as a vehicle for revealing the mind of the Father. Some make much of the peace of God (Phil. 4:7) as an arbiter or umpire in the heart. Peace, or the lack of it, is often used as a means of ascertaining God's will. Without doubt, a deep sense of the rightness of things is a healthy by-product of obedience to the Spirit and the Word and of being in His will, but at the same time we need to guard against the false peace of a dull and insensitive conscience.

b. Guidance by the Spirit is not something separate from one's experience as a member of the body of Christ. In other words, the Lord often reveals His mind through a group of believers rather than just to one member of a group. Acts 13:1–4 is a good example of this kind of guidance, where the Holy Spirit spoke corporately to the group who was worshipping the Lord and gave directions as to two of the number present. As usual, no description is given to satisfy the psychologically curious, but the Lord's call to Barnabas and Saul was a conviction shared by all present and this must have strengthened them both immeasurably as they faced the unknown future. This very method of revealing His will must also greatly have helped to bind them to each other in the bonds of sacrificial prayer.

Surely this is the ideal for all who are being set aside

for special service by the local church. If the call is of God, then often the Lord will reveal this fact to others beside the one being called. Indeed, as a definite seal on one's calling it would be wise to seek this confirmation. Each local church should, in fact, be a guiding body in this sense; but failing the privilege of such fellowship, the called would be wise to seek the counsel and prayer of individual men and women whose spirituality and maturity in the things of the Spirit he can trust. Also compare Acts 15:1-3 with Galatians 2:2, where Paul speaks of going to Jerusalem by 'revelation' although he was sent by elders!

There are Christian organisations that refuse to make any major decisions unless the whole corporate body shares the same conviction. Lobbying is out of order. The ideal is not just gaining a majority by a much-vaunted democratic method either; they believe that the Lord can bring a whole group to one mind and that, failing such unanimity, it is folly to proceed further. Waiting together before the Lord in such a matter can be most profitable for all concerned and on occasion calls for much patience. For further information, reference might be made to Norman Grubb's book *Touching the Invisible*.[1]

c. Guidance by the Spirit is not necessarily apart from circumstance. From a comparison of passages such as Acts 16:6-10 and Galatians 4:13, it may be inferred that to Paul physical sickness could be something permitted by the Spirit to prevent him moving out of the Lord's directive will. The Galatians heard the gospel in the measure they did because Paul's sickness delayed his journeying elsewhere. Further, the introduction of Luke as a companion to Paul in his travels has usually been taken as a key to Paul's vision for Europe.

d. Guidance by the Spirit is not apart from sanctified human judgment. In Acts 15:36 Paul suddenly decides to visit believers in regions where he has previously preached the gospel. His guidance here, without doubt, arose out of the desire for effective 'follow-up'. It is guidance arising from a sense of someone's need and the fact of some capacity to meet it. In a sense, the Macedonian call was of a similar nature, but it needed a special vision to make Paul conscious of the need of peoples who were out of his immediate sense of responsibility. The Holy Spirit remains the master strategist in missions and He can be trusted to manœuvre circumstances as well as the commissioned. A study of the biographies of missionaries such as Livingstone or Joy Ridderhof will further confirm the fact that such things as international strife or personal sickness can all be a means of getting the Lord's servant to the place of His appointing and where the major task is to be done.

1 Samuel 7:1–10 records an interesting illustration of how, in the school of guidance, extraordinary guidance gives place to the use of Saul's own growing sense of commission and he is commanded to 'do as occasion serve thee' (1 Sam. 10:7, A.V.). When young in the faith, some people may on occasion experience phenomenal interventions by the Lord in one way or another. However, this will give way more and more to a steady faithful walk with the Lord where we no longer need the spectacular and manifest to guide us. An exception to this, of course, will be when we are being led to do something utterly different and peculiar to our experience to date. Peter needed a threefold vision before he could be persuaded to use the keys of the kingdom that opened the gospel door to the Gentile world.

One of the dangers of maturity is that we tend to limit God to the measure of our previous experience of Him. Assured knowledge becomes a hindrance to richer experience, for God Himself is so much vaster than the experience of any one of us.

In the contention in Acts 15:39, the first debate on the suitability of a missionary candidate, it is evident that sanctified human judgment played no small part in the ultimate decision. Perhaps both Barnabas and Paul were right in the end, but Paul is the idealist and cannot bear the thought of Mark's previous defection being the cause of stumbling to young Christians where they have previously travelled. To some, Paul is somewhat severe and over-zealous in his judgment, but 'better zeal with ignorance than knowledge with disobedience'.

Paul's very zeal in the Lord's service calls for special comment, for it obviously affected the way in which he was guided. In Acts 16 he had to be checked twice from some projected course of action till he was assured that, after all, Europe was the Lord's call. It is easy to guide a moving ship. It is better to be guided by restraint than passively to await some heavenly visitation that leaves no room for the exercise of discernment. Armchair guidance might permit some movement, but certainly no advance.

e. Guidance by the Spirit is never apart from some didactic purpose. We are apt to become very impatient with God's timing. We may, for instance, feel a clear call to foreign missionary work and yet find ourselves delayed by sickness or some family responsibilities. Our disappointment may be God's appointment—an appointment to training of a highly specialised character. He has much to teach us in the interim; indeed, has God any interims? Every moment of every day is charged with potential significance.

Miss Burnett, whom we have already mentioned, felt called to the mission field while quite young, but because she was housekeeper and secretary to her widowed father, who was in the Anglican ministry, she felt she could not leave home. Rather than lament the fact, however, she gave herself to the ministry that lay around her and specially took to training her mind by committing to memory the record of all the names and addresses of the members of her father's large parish. When at thirty-nine she eventually was able to leave for the mission field, she was able to tackle what is declared to be the world's most difficult language, and in addition there was a maturity about her life and ministry that had much to do with the way God honoured her capable work and used her to found what is now a self-supporting denomination among the Japanese.

In contrast to this, Abraham could not await the gradual unfolding of God's promised purposes for his family and stooped to fleshly expedients to hurry God up! All his subsequent descendants have paid dearly for it ever since. Paget Wilkes, quoting Stuart Holden, recorded the following in his Bible:

> Many an overwhelming mistake has been made, not because God's guidance was not desired, but because it was not waited for. For to take any step apart from unmistakable indication of His approval is to court disaster. No man who tarries His leisure finds himself outstripped by opportunity; for the clouds always lift at the moment most favourable to safe advance. Refusal to move until they do, is highest wisdom.

Guidance is also by circumstance

a. In summary, it can be said that we are guided by circumstance, but not apart from the Bible, the Holy Spirit and waiting upon the Lord in prayer. Joshua 9 has recorded for us the story of the subtlety of the Gibeonites who saved their skins by presuming upon the faithfulness of the Israelites to their own promises. Circumstances alone seemed so clearly to point to the line of duty and so Joshua completely failed to seek the mind of the Lord about these strange visitors. Circumstantial guidance alone is not sufficient.

Alexander Hay, in his interesting book on New Testament principles in missionary work, tells of a local church being invited to hold meetings in a nearby town by someone they had come to trust.[2] It seemed at the outset like a golden opportunity for some pioneering in a new area, but the young church gave itself to prayer and could get no assurance to proceed. Only subsequently did they discover that the person who invited them was living a life so notorious in the neighbourhood, that the influence of any meetings in his home would have been crippled from the outset.

b. Circumstantial guidance will not be without divinely ordained stops and starts. According to George Müller, the stops as well as the steps of a good man are ordained by the Lord. Numbers 9 : 15ff. is full of lessons in this regard, for the children of Israel journeyed only when the cloud moved. Lack of guidance forward was, therefore, very real guidance to stay just where they were! I have found that often the command to move forward in a new direction is preceded by a very definite closing of doors behind or the stirring up of the nest in some way that makes the move advisable.

Fred Mitchell pointed out that if 'we are desirous of doing His will, He will not allow us to get out of it by a small mistake on our part. Rather, He will move heaven and earth to prevent such a calamity.'[3] A passage from the little booklet, *His thoughts said . . . His Father said . . .*, comes readily to mind in this regard :

> Would an earthly father leave a willing child in doubt about his wishes? How much less would thy heavenly Father do so unkind a thing? Must the decision be made today? Then there will be a sign from Me today. Can the matter be deferred? Then there shall be a going on in quietness. Before action must be taken, I will cause something to happen that will show the way of My choice. Though part

of himself be rent, there will be a peace that not even the rending can hurt. There will not be the torment of uncertainty.[4]

I recall the night when the divine intervention of a telegram changed the whole course of my life. After graduation from Bible college and some subsequent Christian service, there was increasing pressure to commit myself to a life work. Just at that time, an opening for work occurred that was most attractive to me and for which many gave willing endorsement. The application was made, but it was finally decided to make no appointments at the time.

I was puzzled. I continued in prayer, however, but at the same time the urge for some action was upon me and when another position for something of the same nature occurred, I asked for the papers. These had to be filled in by a certain deadline and as I did not have real assurance that this was of the Lord I waited till the very last night, trusting that some token one way or the other would give indubitable evidence of His will. I recall actually scrutinising the papers again, still reluctant to fill them in, when the telephone rang. It was a telegram. The substance was to the effect that I was being asked to consider Christian work among students as a staff worker.

I was flabbergasted. Finding it rather difficult to believe that this might be the hoped-for, eleventh-hour intervention of the Lord, I rang up a fellow-student from the university where I had been studying and who had actually once mooted the possibility of such a position to me. I now wondered if there had been some well-intentioned work behind the scenes to help the Lord and me at the same time! My friend was party to nothing of the kind, but rejoiced in the request that had been made. With some more assurance that this was of Him, I turned to my reading for the night and it proved to be the passage in Acts 16 : 1–10, where Paul had twice been restrained by the Holy Spirit from a certain course of action and then while waiting, no doubt in some bewilderment, the vision came from Troas that opened the door of the gospel to Europe. The twofold restraint and then the last-moment intervention seemed to be so akin to my own experience in broad outline that my increasing feelings of utter incapacity for such a task were overwhelmed by the conviction that this was indeed of Him.

I later learned that on that same night the executive officers of the movement were meeting to pray about this very appointment many miles away and my name was broached, but had been laid aside because of some knowledge of the previously mentioned applications. Decision was made to go ahead in contacting me, however, and then one of them said words to this effect: 'Well, let's send a telegram now!' Who prompted him to suggest that? Surely the very One who would not have us in the torment of uncertainty and who well knew that again and again in the future, I would need to look back to the fact of guidance that showed that He could engineer circumstance when and where it was needed.

c. Circumstantial guidance is not apart from human help, but it is not dependent upon it. We find a salutary lesson about this in the story of the prophet in 2 Kings 13, for, after having explicit directions from the Lord Himself, he is willing to listen to contrary advice from the lips of another professed prophet. The sudden and sad demise of the true prophet, rather than that of the false, may seem to us to be strange justice today, but disobedience to the plain Word of God is ever more culpable in the Lord's true servant than deceit in the heart of the false.

In an Eastern culture the young Christian is more subject to direction from his parents and friends than his counterpart in the West. Indeed, when it comes to marriage, in most circles it is still thought wiser to abide by the opinions of relatives or one's pastor than to exercise personal judgment to any extent. However, it is just here that if the adviser happens to have the wrong motives or be mistaken in judgment, his opinion if followed can play havoc with the whole future of the person concerned.

Our dearest friends or relatives or the most revered pastor can never take the place of the Holy Spirit in our walk with God. This is not to argue in favour of an occidental approach to guidance in the matter of a partner in life. I firmly believe that the Lord is able to guide and overrule despite the seeming complexity of customs that would appear to stultify individual choice. But ultimately the person concerned needs to be quite sure that the path suggested is the one that commends itself to his conscience and is consistent with the Word of God. Anything else he has the right to and the responsibility of refusing outright.

I remember the bewilderment that followed the advice of greatly respected Christian friends in regard to my going abroad as a missionary. No doubt with good reason at the time, many argued in favour of work at home. Finally, returning deeply distressed from conversation with one whose opinion I valued most highly, I knelt at my bedside, opening the Bible at the passage for that particular night, which happened to be Genesis 12. God's command to leave country, kindred and father's house and go to a country that He would reveal was like a personal message to me that night and gave me the courage to step out in faith. The decision to move forward was confirmed again and again subsequently through the Word and not least through the same assurance being given to the same friends whose doubt turned to a vital fellowship in prayer.

The testings and loneliness that are bound to come to the missionary call for an assurance not just grounded upon the opinion of friends, comforting though that may be. This may sound like a contradiction of the passage dealing with the guidance given by the Spirit through a group of praying people, but in point of fact it merely stresses the danger of a tendency among us all to be too sensitive to the opinions of others. At the same time, this is not to undervalue in any way the great encouragement that can come through the prayers and advice of truly godly friends.

F. B. Meyer in his book on Joshua speaks of the 'bliss of living when our wills blend to His, like perfect words to perfect music' :

> Then trial and sorrow are treated as our Father's messengers but in their winter costume. Then our very infirmities indicate the direction in which we should spend our energies. Then disappointment becomes impossible, because all is God-appointed. Then we always have our way, because God's and ours are one. Then prayer is the discovery of God's plan and a taking hold of His willingness. Then the heart keeps sabbath like a valley enriched by the great mountains on which the storms expend themselves.[5]

This is the rich heritage of the guided.

1. Published by Lutterworth.
2. Alexander Hay, *The New Testament Order for Church and Missionary* (New Testament Missionary Union), p. 458.
3. From Phyllis Thompson, *Climbing on Track* (Lutterworth), a biography of Fred Mitchell.
4. *His thoughts said . . . His Father said* (S.P.C.K.). p. 63.
5. F. B. Meyer, *Joshua and the Hand of Promise* (Marshall, Morgan and Scott), p. 132.

6

The Call to Service

In the New Testament there is no reference to a Christian
'leader'. In fact the only use of the word is with refere-
ence to the blind leading the blind into the ditch (Matt.
15:14)! Instead the word used is *diakonos*, meaning
'minister' or 'servant'.[1] Christ Himself said 'even . . .
the Son of Man came not to be served but to serve'
(Matt. 20:28), and throughout His life showed in practice how leadership should involve service to others.

This was a lesson which the disciples had to learn.
They were eager to serve the Lord, but were sometimes
indifferent to the everyday needs of one another. They
quarrelled about who was to be the greatest in the kingdom while at the same time failing in everyday cour-
tesies, such as washing their Master's feet when they
entered the house for a meal. There should have been a
competition among them as to whose privilege it was
to be next to perform this service, but perhaps they
realised that even if they began with His, it would mean
doing the others' too. His, yes, but not those of others!
The Lord Himself put them in their rightful place by
Himself washing their feet—Judas's included.

Serving with reservations
At one time or another, most of us labour under the

70

delusion that we can serve the Lord without serving our fellowmen. We would not express it that way, of course, but the unwelcome truth is that we can serve the Lord only through people—ordinary, often proud, sometimes ungrateful, and, on occasion, disgusting people.

We can sing,

> *Take my silver and my gold.*
> *Not a mite would I withhold.*

and Jesus is quite likely to say to us, 'Then what about deliberately sharing some of the silver with the poor folk you know, and showing that you know my love by taking active steps to heal the rift between yourself and the people you have avoided for months?' But no, we would prefer an essentially 'spiritual' service that does not involve us in these sordid, sorrowful, mixed-up lives all around us. We want to reap a golden harvest without the drudgery of ploughing the soil of common human interests, and watering the ground with the tears of mutual sorrow.

Borden of Yale was a millionaire who could have worked solely in the upper strata of society. Yet while he was at college preparing for mission service, he could be found at night in a downtown mission with his arm around some poor derelict seeking to lead him to the Saviour. Borden deliberately involved himself in the problem of what makes men the wrecks they are without God.[2]

I confess to my shame that, when invited to such a mission while at Bible college, I was glad to be asked to play the piano for the hymns rather than be expected to get alongside the meths-soaked dregs of society who had merely come to the place for a free feed. Serving the Lord? Yes, but with reservations. I discovered that I was born a Pharisee and only the love of Christ can break these chains of hypocritical religious indifference.

Eugenia Price, in her book *Strictly Personal*,[3] tells of

how her mother was reproached by a hardworking fellow-member of the Women's Christian Temperance Union for not being active in the work of late. Her mother, among other things, countered the rebuke by telling of her practical efforts to win an alcoholic friend. Instead of expected interest the reply was, 'I wouldn't have one of those drunken people in my house for a minute!' Read Joe Bayly's story of the *Gospel Blimp*,[4] a devastating satire on the folly of trying to serve the Lord while ministering to people from a distance.

Serving a mere alternative
Another common fallacy is that of confusing an idea of the Lord's service with the fact of serving the Lord Himself. We can get an idea of Christian service through traditional channels and pursue that idea with diligence, and perhaps even with no little sacrifice, and yet unwittingly be opposed to His essential will for us. The 'idea' may take the concrete form of a mission society or one's local church, and be all the more deceptive for that very reason.

As a member of some mission society for spreading the gospel, for example, we may have pledged ourselves to uphold the society's rules. The very quality of these principles may originally have attracted us but the higher the standard, the more the tendency is for us to get our eyes on the mission and its principles and off the Lord who no doubt first inspired their promulgation. They become, like the law to the Jews, the great alternative. If we are primarily devoted to the Lord then we will 'automatically' keep the principles that are essential to a smooth-working society, but if not, then unconsciously we will find ourselves in bondage to the mere 'letter of the law'.

No missionary is more touchy than the one who is primarily devoted to his mission and for that very reason no missionary is more often offended when the mission 'lets him down'. He is primarily the mission's

servant and so rightly—though unconsciously, perhaps
—expects all his satisfaction and reward and recognition from the mission itself. Further, he will want to be
served by the mission. He will make demands and expect his 'rights' and, in short, will be a constant menace
to the team-work that is so essential on the mission field,
for his primary devotion is to an imperfect instrument
rather than to the Lord Himself.

Admittedly, a Christian's devotion to Christ can conceivably on occasion be measured in terms of his adher-
ence to the aims of the particular Christian group to
which he belongs, whether that group be a mission,
a local church, or a student Christian Union, and in
terms of loyalty to his fellow-members. I always suspect
that the Christian who is volubly critical of his own
group is out of touch with his Lord. If there are things
wrong within one's own group then there is a proper
and helpful way of voicing a protest without spreading one's disquiet like an insidious contagion.

One can see the outworking of some of these problems
in relation to the building of churches in a foreign land.
For example, most of us are heavily conditioned in our
ideas as to the Lord's service before we leave home. The
pattern of church behaviour, prayer language, methods
of conducting the Lord's supper and baptism, keeping
the Lord's day and other similar habits are usually
established norms after centuries of Christianity-cum-
churchianity in the West.

On the positive side, because we have been blessed by
our own home church we tend to feel that any church
brought into being through our labours abroad should
have the same emphases, for otherwise we are not preaching the 'full gospel' and Christians will not grow. On the
negative side, we may have joined a mission society
that has emphases in the opposite direction from that
of our own home church and is all the more attractive
for that very reason! But the tendency then is for us to
go to an opposite extreme. For example, we might fail

adequately to teach the meaning of baptism for the simple reason that our own home church has emphasised the subject to the point of baptismal regeneration. Or, because our own mission society makes no appeal for funds, we fail to teach young converts to give or support their national fellow-workers in a practical way.

It is regrettable that so much missionary endeavour and church building on the part of the foreigner gives every indication of mere devotion to traditional foreign forms. The very occidental or at least exotic shape of church buildings, foreign-inspired church vestments, local words slavishly set to foreign tunes, and an order of church service can all be pathetically remote from both the needs of the local Christians and the healthy indigenous tradition that could conceivably have been theirs. Even a certain demeanour that is common to Christians of any one communion at home is apt to be duplicated in astonishing measure by Christians of the same communion abroad, especially in a country like Japan where mimicry is a fine art.

On arriving in Japan, at our first port of call, we stepped off the ship to gaze around and to my astonishment and joy found a church with the name of my own denomination written across the door—in English. Just then the young pastor stepped out and on seeing us probably realised we were missionaries and invited us in. Amidst all the tumbled first impressions that remain so vividly with me, even to the feeling of embarrassment at having to leave my shoes in the entrance, the thing that staggered me was to realise that though this young pastor could hardly speak a word of English, yet the cut of his clothes, the kind and colour of his tie, and indeed his whole demeanour shouted aloud that he could have graduated from my home church theological college just the year before. Since then, as part of a rather melancholy game, I have been compelled to note how Japanese Christians are so often true to form—not a simple biblical form being expressed in a way that makes them essentially Christian in their own environment, but an exotic form that makes them both foreign as well as Christian. The end result is a plant that is difficult to cultivate.

It would seem, therefore, that missionaries have come to the foreign field serving the Lord through their church or mission society and for that very reason have not been free enough in spirit to see that perhaps the Lord's pattern for His Church in this country is something in some respects as yet foreign to their own experience and background and imagination. They were primarily the Church's servant, or at best, a servant of one of its branches, but not the servant of its Head, and thus failed to be sufficiently sensitive to people's real needs.

One of the reasons for the amazing spread of the new religions in Japan is that the cults have a genius for adaptation to the needs, aspirations and the very vocabulary of the ordinary person. Some of their methods are completely neutral as to moral or ethical content but with uncanny precision have been taken up by masters of mass psychology and applied to their own ends with effect. In contrast to this, the Church in so many of its branches seems to be anything but a healthy plant flourishing in local soil. Slavish addiction to the forms and approach of the revered foreign founders can create a decided rut, which, as someone has said, is only a grave with both ends removed!

A missionary came to visit us and I discovered he was an isolated member of a small splinter group just arrived in Japan from the West. He very soon asked me what we were doing about church building and when I countered with the same question found him not so hesitant in replying. I discovered that he had a small brochure attached to the back of his Bible that set out the aims and structure of the church he intended to build. He confessed that he was not good at explaining things but it was all there for him to follow. Here was a pre-fabricated job, fabricated abroad with the best of intentions and about to be superimposed upon any group of believers that might be added to him. In the course of conversation, he remarked condescendingly that he would not go so far as to say that everyone else was wrong, but he knew that he and his particular group were right! In one sense, it could conceivably simplify one's labours to have things so cut and dried. To add to the false sense of achievement, I am sure he will find some who are glad to submit their conscience and will to someone who seems to know so very definitely what the will of God is, for there is a real sense of security in just toeing the line. If and when the missionary leaves, however, and the Christian who is left has to go direct to the Word of God with all his problems, he might come up with some different answers. Usually, when the prop is removed then the building collapses.

Paul said, 'You are serving the Lord Christ.' While thankful for all that the home church has come to mean and all that it has contributed to one's understanding of the Bible as it is applied to a Western culture, our primary devotion must be centred in Christ Himself and obedience to Him, for only then are we free enough from mere tradition to be willing to serve in a new capacity, submit to the guidance of Christians in another culture, and do things in the best interests of the local church that would never have entered the head of the experienced exegete at home.

A conditioned service
Another common fallacy is that we can serve the Lord conditionally. Christian workers on occasion give the impression that they are working on a forty-hour-week plan, a kind of spiritual labour union whereby we give so many hours to the 'boss' and the rest of the time is ours. We would never say that, of course, but it becomes evident enough when we reflect upon the way we are tempted to treat those who infringe upon 'our' time, and we do not take kindly to 'being imposed upon'.

We pity ourselves when our will or inclination is crossed or personal plans upset by a request from someone over us in the Lord, or by some young Christian who seems to imagine that we have time to spare and would be specially delighted to be able to spend it all with him! The young Christian, as it happens, in the full glow of a new-found faith and naïvety of an unspoilt zeal for Jesus, cannot imagine a Christian leader who is not always at his people's disposal, and always rejoicing at the opportunity of unfolding more of the riches of the Word of God.

The Lord's prayer times seem frequently to have been interrupted. When He was tired He was disturbed by a fallen woman or by some raging storm, or He was frustrated in doing some good deed by having to do another, and yet you never get any sense of fretting or impatience or broken plans in His gloriously full life and ministry. 'I am among you as one who serves,' He said (Luke 22:27), and Paul, following hard in his Lord's steps, could speak of gladly spending and being spent for the Corinthian believers (2 Cor. 12:15). Christians who have impressed me the most have been those who seem to be completely at rest from themselves and thus able to devote all their energies to meeting the needs of others. They seem to be tuned in, so to speak, and therefore attract needy people to themselves. Real sympathy will find a whole world of problems right at hand to drink it dry.

Some of us, in sad contrast to this, appear to be mere professionals. Our service is a 'thus-far-and-no-further' approach. We carefully dole out our interest and energy, being careful to leave enough of the latter to follow our own congenial interests—when we can be 'free'. This lack of real heart in our service and real concern for the individual is detected intuitively by both Christian and non-Christian alike, and for that very reason we are left alone to enjoy our mess of pottage. In the East, however, because as missionaries we are recognised as teachers, or because we hold some position of oversight and therefore should be respected, and not because of our essential spiritual calibre, people are obliged to seek our help and this can serve to give a superficial assurance that we are 'serving the Lord'.

Under the same heading, we might say something about the fallacy of thinking we can serve the Lord without being told what to do! The leader of one missionary society suggested that there were too many missionary statesmen on the mission field and what they needed was more followers. Most of us, fortunately, do not suffer from megalomania and often feel the need of some direction and want to be led personally by the Lord Himself. What we do find difficult to tolerate is getting orders from the Lord through one of His servants! As Winston Churchill has well said, we want to learn, but we do not like being taught. Certainly as a final-year student we perhaps find it difficult to accept ideas from someone who has just come up to college and who has retained the zeal of school Christian life. Occasionally, for the sake of our pride and His own glory, God delights to distil wisdom from the mouths of babes in experience. On the mission field we have to be willing to learn through some young national Christian whose local insight into the things of God has not been spoiled by Western pedantry or accommodated to Western custom.

Excessive individualism, while perhaps the secret of material success in a society dedicated to free enterprise, is one characteristic of the Westerner that is neither palatable to the homogeneous Oriental whose passion it is to conform, nor is it helpful to the growth of a local church where the individual, like a single cell in the human body, can only neglect its part in the whole at the cost of turning malignant. Some of us, because of inability to adjust to this topsy-turvy Oriental world and rightly assess where we could make perhaps a modest but certainly a positive contribution to the growth of the Church, prefer to specialise in some ministry we feel most fitted to our own special gifts.

Lafcadio Hearn, a Greek who became a naturalised Japanese and was once a lecturer at Tokyo University, has declared that philosophical forms of Japanese society have nothing in common with those of the West; and Francis Xavier felt that the Japanese language was invented by the devil in order to prevent the spread of the gospel! But these problems are nothing compared with the frustration of coming to a country with preconceived ideas of service that we will not modify in the face of new circumstances or opportunity. For this reason, some have left the council of experienced men or the fellowship of fellow-workers in order to labour alone. Devoted to our own ideas of service, we can bustle around erecting buildings, and with paid national help we may eventually have something to show for all the outlay of energy, that is until the shock of reality and shifting circumstance reveal just how shallow the work really is. The solitary corn of wheat has to die to the desire to be so solitary, before, with others, it brings forth its manifold harvest.

I confess that before coming to the mission field I had a very inadequate conception of service in the Church. Much of the time I was merely a fellow-passenger, a sponge to soak up all I could get with little thought of washing believers' feet! If the Bible class members were irreverent and inattentive then I told them off, not just because they were insulting God by their behaviour, but also because they were wasting my valuable time. Membership in most churches was numerous enough to enable me to steer clear of people who were dull, unfriendly, or apparently not impressed by my spirituality! Bible college and four years of army life taught me some valuable lessons about getting alongside people nearly as odd, and certainly as uncommunicative as myself, but the mission field has introduced me to a whole new realm of service and made me realise as never before how desperately I need the fellowship of other Christians. Submitting to one another in love; trusting not to prestige nor to the weight of leadership prerogatives, but to the authority that truth alone will give to those who walk openly in the light; asking how one can help instead of waiting to be asked; anticipating the needs of others and supplying them in a way that may never be discovered; rebuking the careless in the interest of their highest good—but with leaden feet; spending time with those who do not stimulate but leave you like a piece of chewed string; sharing experiences of the Lord's personal dealing that bursts any bubble of pride but brings you right alongside others in similar trouble: these and many other ways can be an expression of a togetherness that does help us to grow up into maturity in Christ as serving members of His body— the Church.

Weymouth's brilliant rendering of Ephesians 4:16 will suffice as a conclusion: 'Dependent on Him, the whole body—its various parts closely fitting and firmly adhering to one another—grows by the aid of every contributory link with power proportioned to the need of each individual part, so as to build itself up in a spirit of love.'

1. See, e.g. 1 Cor. 3:5; 2 Cor. 3:6; Eph. 3:7; Col. 1:7, 23; 1 Tim. 4:6.
2. See Mrs Howard Taylor, *Borden of Yale* (Overseas Missionary Fellowship).
3. Published by Zondervan.
4. Published by Victory Press.

7

Identification

The days of Hudson Taylor's artificial pigtail are over, but alas, the reaction of some foreign missionaries towards his efforts to be identified with the Chinese is still with us. The kind of desegregation needed will never be introduced by a supreme court ruling or mission society principles, for it is a matter of heart willingness to be as closely at one with a new people as is consistent with one's calling among them.

That calling Jesus stressed in His prayer in John 17:18, 'As thou didst send me, so I have sent them'. The word 'as' can yield a number of interesting meanings, but it can hardly bear detailed application to the measure of the infinite stoop of His incarnation. We cannot even conceive of the glory that He left behind! Our being sent into the world can hardly mirror all that it meant for God to assume flesh, nor can we touch the mere hem of His sacrificial garments when He died a sufficient offering for the sins of all mankind. Yet there is something about that identification with mankind which, in spirit at least, must be in the heart of each Christian worker if we are to fulfil our commission. Naturally the mission field is the most obvious place where adjustments have to be made, and hence the following illustrations with that background, but the principles of identification apply wherever a servant of God is anxious to communicate effectively with the non-Christian.

One significance of the Lord's coming was that God's final message came to us in warm, living flesh. He, as Frank Boreham has put it so well, was the pronunciation of the unpronounceable Word! God Himself visited us in bodily form so that His thoughts might become clearly audible, His will graphically intelligible, and His Person fully understandable. The Word must become flesh. And so it is today, for as one veteran missionary has said, 'God's best missionary method is still incarnation.'

We are sent, therefore, not drawn. The 'need of the heathen' will result in as effective an identification as the condescension lampooned in *The Ugly American*.[1] No, we are sent to embody the Word; not to 'blast them with the gospel', as I heard one missionary revealingly describe his ministry, but to adorn the doctrine of God our Saviour in all things, in a life that demonstrates just how deeply and persistently God cares.

In one sense, fortunately, our very differences and limitations as foreign missionaries are an opportunity to demonstrate the essential meaning of why we have been sent to a strange culture with an even stranger message. Our lack of facility in the language of the people can further serve to add weight to deeds prompted by a love that is the world's universal tongue. Acts of simple thoughtfulness can tellingly betray a heart that is at rest from itself and free to serve anyone in need. A lady missionary asked a Japanese evangelist who was visiting the mission headquarters if he had a shirt that she could wash for him. He had been on a caravan mission for some time with foreigners as their interpreter and helper, and had visited many different missionary homes, but this was the first time anyone had asked to help him in such a personal way—and especially a foreigner! He was so staggered that he did present a dirty shirt just to see, as he said later, if she really meant it, which fortunately she did. This was one of the links that encouraged him later to become a member of that particular mission.

A limited identification

In many cultures it would be quite unwise for the missionary to try to 'go native'. In the case of a married man with wife and family, it would be almost impossible if they are to maintain good health and rear the children in the atmosphere they need. On the other hand, in highly civilised countries like Japan, the missionary may, depending upon the district where he lives, be living on a lower plane than his neighbours.

Customs

The incidental customs of life need not make a fundamental difference if the heart is right. Miss Burnett was a woman of huge proportions who could not sit on the floor, never mind bow with her head to the floor to greet guests as is the custom in Japan. She maintained a stolidly British way of life, but this did not seem to bother her loyal Japanese workers, for her heart was so transparently with them. Fellow foreign workers were apt to be distressed at the preference she always gave to the Japanese in her thinking. They themselves had to take second place and apparently did not always like it.

On the other hand, most of us are not sensitive enough as to what might unnecessarily hurt the feelings of the cultured of another race. Watch a missionary react to traditional codes of Japanese courtesy. Does he take advantage of the prevailing privileges of what is pre-eminently a man's country and at the same time, is he too 'busy' to show the usual overwhelming hospitality to guests? Is he unwilling to master the traditional honorific language forms in order to address people consistent with their station in life? Or, just because it is so ultra-Eastern, is he for ever fulminating against the custom of having to weigh nicely with appropriate gifts the measure of every social obligation? Most of these habits of life that have become second nature to the Japanese are perfectly harmless in themselves, but they can be decidedly irksome to the missionary with a Western chip on his shoulder.

A missionary family known to me are living in a Western-style home. This is not now so strange a sight in the cities where they are forsaking traditional forms. But the major difference here is that the children are allowed to run inside with their shoes on. The Japanese would overlook this, too, perhaps if it were not for the reason given: that the missionaries did not want their children to return home later like *yabanjin* (savages)! Judging by the usual behaviour of foreign children in public here, the boot is very definitely on the other foot. Missionaries can be so wedded to a Western way of life that even when foreign customs are superior they will be religiously rejected.

Possessions
Missionaries have been embarrassed by the sheer kindness of well-meaning friends who have determined to see that they have every Western convenience to aid them in life and ministry abroad and it has often resulted in homes well above the average. A Japanese non-Christian visited such a missionary in the 1950s and after gazing around at the size of the rooms, the furniture, the carpets, the giant-sized refrigerator and the like, very candidly remarked that he, too, would like to be a Christian! I do not blame him. Another missionary of a denominational society confessed to me that the size of their dwelling gave the neighbours a false impression and militated against his desire to commence cottage meetings.

A missionary friend sold his station wagon because he was sensitive enough to feel that the public image he was creating by its use put him in a wage-bracket that was untrue, and he was being robbed of opportunities of meeting people on their own level. This is not to say that for certain types of ministry and in certain places such as the bigger cities, such a vehicle cannot be a tremendous asset without creating any false impression. What impressed me was the willingness of this man to do without something which was a must to many foreign missionaries at that time. That same missionary now has a station wagon again because times have so drastically changed and his work warrants it.

In the matter of holding possessions lightly, Japanese will probably make better missionaries to their fellow-Orientals and we can see the Lord's wisdom in thrusting forth an increasing number of Japanese to Laos, Vietnam, India and so on. Theirs is a greater detachment from things; they are more used to a simple form of life and are less addicted to fastidious tastes in diet. The Lord knew what He was about. As Dean of a Bible college, He Himself had no pillow for His head, and the treasurer was a thief. The pupils were for ever quarrelling as to who was to get the best job on graduation. Pity their passions then if they had graduated from some of the Bible colleges of the indulgent West! George Macdonald suggested that 'when a man begins to abstain, then first he recognises the strength of his passion : it may be, when a man has not a thing left, he will begin to know what a necessity he had made of things'.[2]

Time
Many of us find the Eastern conception of time requires a major adjustment. I have been in many gatherings where the foreigner is the first one to look at his watch, either to enquire about the next meal or a suitable train. Orientals obviously are quite intrigued by our devotion to the god Morpheus. Missionaries will visibly sigh at the prolongation of an evening meeting. To be frank, for them it has been just one more meeting but to some, at least, of the Japanese present, it has been far from

prosaic and far from long! All week they are surrounded by forces utterly hostile to faith, and this fellowship time is often all too brief for their lonely lives. In typical Oriental fashion, at the conclusion of the meeting they are just beginning to get to the place where they can open up and share what is really on their hearts.

One missionary is known among the Japanese for his faithfulness to promises to his wife to be home by a certain time. He may be even counselling a church member and yet he has to cut it short to be home on time. To him no doubt this is some kind of a virtue but to the Japanese it seems like utter bondage. I had to come to a Buddhist-saturated society to learn that the world does not come to an end if we do not eat a meal when it is hot and just served—and on time. Many of us have never fasted until we got to the mission field and then it has not been of our choosing. It would be better if we had practised it voluntarily before we came, or at least disciplined our appetites to the point that the occasional prolongation of a meeting did not leave us both gastronomically and vocally protesting about the needs of the inner man.

We are sent to minister to a people of another culture and it is for us as guests to adjust to their way of life in anything that does not involve compromising the Word of God. For this reason we have little right to talk about them wasting our time—as though we had any time we could call our own. A Japanese guest comes when we are in the midst of preparing a message and, in Oriental fashion, he does not hurry to get to the point; we must spend time with him on conventional trivialities. On our part we will not identify ourselves effectively with the nationals unless other people's needs are a major concern to us and we are free from those inflexible schedules we nail to the wall of our intentions.

College students have taught me the same lesson. We often meet during a lunch hour when the time is short and I try to give time for questions at the end of a message but am often met by that 'Why so sudden?' bewilderment and I have gone home frustrated. On their own initiative the same students have arranged special meetings for questions, held at a more leisurely time with biscuits and tea, and I am invited to attend—'not to preach' I am told, but to be there for questions. Those questions then come tumbling out fast and I have a wonderful time preaching as I answer questions. It calls for an identification with their schedules, their moods, their own heart's questions and their leadership —then the opportunities come.

Total identification
The kind of total identification that is needed involves the Word hurting us where it should and can hurt others, for we cannot preach it effectively unless it is evident that we are also trembling at its authority. Some missionaries never confess to failure or ask for prayer in case they lose the nationals' respect. Both they and the nationals are the losers, for it is reality that is going to give the Word its cutting edge. It is a double-edged sword.

Old Testament prophets always stagger me by the measure in which they identified themselves with their message and the coming judgment they usually depicted. They had personally to demonstrate their message. One is commanded not to marry, another to welcome back a faithless wife and another is not permitted even to shed a tear at the sudden death of his beloved. You can see the aristocratic Isaiah walking the streets of the city for three years with bare feet, and others dramatise the coming judgment upon an apostate Israel in ways that turn you off your food to think of them.

Moses was not called upon merely to dramatise the fate of a disobedient Israel, however, but so to associate himself with his people's guilt that he was willing to be cursed in their place, rather than that Yahweh should create a new tribe from his own progeny. There is something lacking in a missionary's commission, therefore, when the national Christians are referred to, often derogatively, by the impersonal pronoun 'they' and 'them'. Identification has not yet reached the place of 'we' and 'us'. That kind of identification does not involve a change of citizenship unless it be to realise in fact that our citizenship is in heaven.

Admittedly, the very age in which we live militates against this kind of thing. It is an age of limited identification and truncated commissions. It is an age when the very affluence of the West enables Christians to take holidays touring the mission fields in luxurious cruisers—painless observation of places where all too few are really travailing for the birth of a healthy church. It is the jet age when we rarely find a whole life dedicated to the lasting benefit of another race, which involves long-term planning that takes failing health or international strife as merely incidental to the fulfilment of a divine imperative. Men want an impersonal ministry and a limited identification. Some missionaries are said never really to unpack. Perhaps we are too firmly wedded to the civilisation that we have left behind, not realising that both it as well as Communism will be as the feet of clay described in Daniel, which disintegrate before the stone cut without hands.

The Millions' recorded the incident of the send-off of Japanese missionaries to Laos:

> The aged father of one of these missionaries had stood on the wharf among the great crowd of Christians who had gathered there to bid the young men farewell. An American missionary came to sympathise with the father and said,
>
> 'Honourable Sir, you must feel this parting very keenly, but be of good cheer, you will see your son again when he returns to Japan for furlough.'
>
> The old father replied,
>
> 'Pastor, when we Japanese sent our sons to the

war and saw them go overseas to fight for their country, we did not expect to see them again. In fact, we told them—do not return again; give your life for your country! Now I am sending this young son of mine across the seas to another and more glorious conflict—to the service of the King of Kings. Should I hope to see him again on the shores of Japan? No; we give him gladly to service in Laos, and we do not expect to see him again on this earth.'

The identification that costs
A Japanese missionary couple in Thailand whom I know are praying about taking out Thai citizenship in order to associate themselves more adequately with Thai people. That kind of identification is probably never even contemplated by Western missionaries and it is not because the Japanese are less proud of their own race and its 2,000 years' culture.

I have known a missionary go to absurd lengths to be 'indigenous' with little known effect except perhaps on his own discomfort, and certainly that of his poor wife! I know how sensitive the Oriental is to empty show, for outward conformity without the inward identification is a tinkling symbol that merely advertises its worthlessness.

The love that involves itself to the hilt in the betterment of the whole person; a home where everyone can be sure of a warm welcome—at all hours; a person-to-person ministry without a smell of professionalism or pride: these and other such wholesome evidences of God's love in us, will, I know, step confidently over all the barriers of culture, and make us as at one with people of another race as it is possible, and justifiable to be. This is the identification that costs.

Now all this would be so much 'pigs might fly' if it were not that the stimulus and motivation for this kind of life were not exactly the same as that of the Lord

Himself. Again and again throughout His ministry you catch the note of dependence upon His Father. He did nothing on His own volition. His words and works were given Him from above—it was a life of utter dependence. Then He tells us that just as He was sent, so are we. It makes all the difference who sends us. A lad sent on an errand by his favourite teacher is treading on air; the journey is too short and the difficulties a privilege. We are sent ones of the Lord Himself, and just as an essential part of His ministry was His identification with a fallen race, so an essential part of our ministry is our identification with others till we see Christ formed in them. With the willingness to obey there will come the enabling.

1. W. J. Lederer and E. L. Burdick, *The Ugly American* (Gollancz).
2. See *George Macdonald, An Anthology*, edited by C. S. Lewis (Geoffrey Bles).
3. A periodical of the Overseas Missionary Fellowship.

<h1 style="text-align:center">8</h1>

The First Prerogative

The Christian, and the leader in particular, has one undeniable prerogative. It is to die. If he lives long enough, he will probably die a thousand deaths!

Christians of an earlier generation often spoke about a cross that involved the death of the believer. Today we call them the mystics, but that of which they spoke was decidedly real. To Paul, the crucifixion was not just the main theme of his preaching. He spoke of himself as crucified *with* Christ. We cannot preach the one effectively without experiencing the other.

Today much is made of an objective, historical, crucified Jesus, by whom we are saved. But the cross that is so focal to history as the supreme revelation of God's saving work must also become subjective—a principle of life within us. It is the principle of life out of death. What God has done for us in the death of Jesus His Son continues to be done in us by the same principle, resulting in a constant experience of death to the self-life, for we are salvaged by liquidation!

Someone has suggested that if we cover nothing, defend nothing and excuse nothing, we will find out just how deeply entrenched the self-life is. We are, therefore, called not only to forsake our sins when we come to Jesus Christ, but from then on, to forsake our self-life daily, for the Lord does not offer simply an improved animal life and certainly not just some first lessons in the psychology of sublimation. He offers life out of death.

Jesus Himself presaged His own death in that memorable word-picture of the grain of wheat falling into the ground in John 12:24. The seed is lost to its 'self'. It loses its essential form. In order to become food for the developing new life it suffers drastic changes in nature. Its very essence is lost and absorbed to give life to something greater. If not, it merely abides alone.

In commenting upon these verses a young Japanese Christian remarked that we are not asked to die on *tatami*—that is, the smooth padded floor of the living rooms in a Japanese house that is treated much like the top of the dining-room table in the West. This death is no social occasion. There will be no family condolence and certainly nothing of all that goes to make a martyrdom! It is death of another kind—hidden in the earth. It is not necessarily life poured out and prematurely terminated by excess of zeal, for in the midst of zeal itself, self has its servants for self-preservation. This death is a deliberate act of a tutored will, whereby the Christian is able increasingly to say 'no' to every selfish impulse of the self-life and to welcome every implication of what it means for the Lord to reign within.

Self-life and the instincts
Nowhere is the self-life more hydra-headed and more deeply entrenched than in the realm of the instincts.

The instinct for self-preservation, for example, is ordinarily a very healthy safeguard against danger to life and limb. Only the mentally sick or utterly despairing throw themselves in front of trains! However, the very strength of this instinct in a healthy person adds fixity to bondage when the desire is to preserve one's self for one's self alone. Only the impulse of great affection is sufficient to break these bonds of a nature turned within itself. That sacrifice a Quaker lady once described as the ecstasy of giving the best we have to the one we love the most. If the Lord is in very truth the centre of a Christian's affections, then much of the battle of the self-life and its initial needed abandonment is over.

Who among us has not at one time and another felt the strongest impulse to vindicate himself? The instinct to preserve our reputation at any cost is rooted deep in our pride. The contradictions of sinners against us is bad enough, but when saints join in the fray it is salt rubbed into the wounds of the one being crucified. However, to triumph here is to assure the Lord's own unmistakable vindication as sure as His crown followed His cross.

On the other hand, any Christian in a position of responsibility is particularly subject to the temptation to live up to some fancied standard consistent with his position of authority, when actually he may have long departed from the very spiritual credentials that brought him into office. A willingness to die to this kind of unreality will strike at the very vitals of spiritual pride and of necessity will often involve a death penalty that is humiliatingly public.

Selfish friendships are rooted in the gregarious instinct. This is a perfectly healthy urge in us all but stronger in some than in others. However it can also lead to exclusive relationships between people of the same sex. This problem is not uncommon at home, and as for the missionaries who are often called upon to live a lonely and unnatural life in a strange country, if there is not a constant finding of all one's joys in the Lord Himself, and a pouring out of one's basic desires on the altar of the needs of the people around, they can develop a friendship that is a bondage rather than a blessing.

Sometimes the Christian worker himself needs a special friend. Yet most of the time he is called to be the good friend of all and the special friend of none. This is a field where Paul's principles of conduct surely apply; see 1 Corinthians 6:12; 10:23, 24. Friendships legitimate? Yes, but he will not be brought under their power. A special friend? Why not? Well, not if it does not build up or edify the body of Christ. Certainly not if fellowship with others is limited by virtue of the habit of confiding in one person alone. Even a husband and wife, if they are not careful, can become very selfish in their oneness. The writer has on more than one occasion had to 'die' to his wife temporarily while attending conferences. It is a mark of grave weakness to the Oriental Christian, if the missionary must always be with his wife whenever he has a spare moment. In point of fact, whatever country we are in, when married couples are together they need to go out of their way to make the unmarried at home in their presence.

Self-assertiveness rises out of the instinctive desire to rule or lord it over others. This seems to be the vice of the 'privileged' few. By this, I mean that some have magnetic gifts of leadership that are by-products of a gifted parentage, not necessarily stemming from the anointing of the Spirit for a specific task. The tragedy is that people of this calibre are often shoved into positions where their 'weight' is needed. Almost invariably they will be men of some success in secular affairs, but in many cases when called upon to act in the realm of the Spirit, they will be influenced by the factors that made them successful in business in the material world. You may run a department store like a mission, but it is doubtful if the reverse is possible! This is no sweeping criticism of men of God who are honoured with success materially because of unswerving principles and who devote their largesse to the spread of the gospel. The writer knows of enough of them to rejoice in its recurring possibility. When a man of great gift but with uncrucified self is placed in an executive position, as was King Uzziah, having outstanding success as an administrator, he sometimes presumes upon the priesthood as well. If King Uzziah had previously died to self-assertiveness and spiritual pride, he would not have been struck with leprosy for his presumption.

A Japanese thinker once described his society to me in terms of *entotsu bunmei*, i.e. chimney civilisation. From some promontory above a major city, the tall chimneys of industrial plants seem to dominate the scene. He suggested that, in like manner, Japanese society was dominated by a few outstanding personalities. Or, to coin the phrase of another teacher, 'We are either dictators or sheep'. In a society still eating the left-overs from feudalism, the common tendency is for pastors to assume extraordinarily wide authoritative powers over members of the congregation. Even in the West, where individualism can on occasion be said to have run amok, spiritual leaders are tempted to assume a role in the church quite beyond the special gifts given them of the Spirit. The leader is at fault where he fails to recognise that the desire to be always wanted and 'used' often lies in an uncrucified self. Somewhat related to the above is the desire to possess, the acquisitive instinct.

When we are wrapped up in ourselves, someone has said that we make very small parcels indeed. But the language is always the same, for out of the abundance of the hoarded material the mouth speaks, even talking of 'my converts'. What presumption that can be! Unless they are just believers in myself, then I am being revealingly truthful. 'My money.' Ah, here we strike trouble with a capital T. On the mission field, for example, it has been found wise in most organisations to separate designated personal funds from those used for the general running of the mission and its personnel and work. Unless the missionary, however, maintains a sensitive stewardship and sits very lightly to 'his' possessions, he can become a drone in the hive. Some prefer to remain independent of organisations in order to handle what they call the 'Lord's money' in a way that they feel is consistent with their special call. With some, this is obviously the right thing to do. But with others, wise restraint and counsel with other people on how best to make use of funds is needed. 'My money' then becomes 'the Lord's money' in a hurry—as conveniently as a *Corban* with an irresponsible Jew.

'*My* time—*my* programme, and that schedule I just *must* meet! Oh, what a nuisance, there goes the door-bell, and I've only begun this prayer letter!' Yes, even if it is my carefully construed idea of how best to spend time for Him, it can still be selfish. Distressingly enough, we often fail to see His appointments in our interruptions. How all-pervasive are the inroads of self!

Many a work of God founders also on the jagged rock of envy, a poison bitter in the hearts of the Pharisees that ultimately hounded Jesus to the cross. But, thank God, that very same cross and Him crucified, is the secret of its neutralisation.

The testimony of those who 'died'
Isobel Kuhn records the frank confession of a missionary friend whose experience was apparently identical with hers: 'The first few years of my service the Lord had to spend in bringing me to an end of myself.' Getting there is no Saturday afternoon excursion for some of us and the 'bigger' we are, the harder we fall! Let us take a look at some of the experiences of Christians through the years in this regard. The words may be different, but the principle is identical.

John Tauler of the fourteenth century was reckoned to be the greatest preacher of his day, but 1331 saw him brought to the place of utter rejection and shame before his own people. At the height of his popularity, Nicholas of Basle had the courage and insight to tell him that the gifted orator must die. The Lord Himself chose the time and place of His servant's 'death' but he was made to drink the bitter cup of humiliation before the crowds of Strasbourg—crowds he had once held in the hollow of his hand. Only then did the Lord take him up and use him as never before.

George Müller was once asked the secret of his phenomenal success in the Christian life and he could only reply that there was a day when he had died—utterly died. To him it meant death to the plaudits and/or the blame of men and a living to please the Lord alone.

John Sung, the apostle to China from 1928 to 1951, would confirm the same thing. He lost his faith in an American seminary and when the Lord suddenly spoke to him like Moses of old, his liberal friends thought he had lost his mind and had him placed in a mental institution for 193 days. He was very sane, however, and with the brilliantly trained mind that was his, he gave himself to unhurried Bible study and later declared that the day of his release was his true graduation! En route home, apart from a trophy kept to please his father, Sung threw his academic prizes overboard. He had died to the promise of a lucrative academic career and determined to live only for Christ. He had a profound influence on his generation.

A. B. Simpson, the founder of the Christian and Missionary Alliance, tells 'of a lonely and sorrowful night when mistaken in many things and imperfect in all, and not knowing but that it would be death in the most literal sense before the morning light' when he made his first full consecration. He trod the lonely path of rejection, and when he began his great work in New York City there were only seven people at the first service.

The point of controversy with God, the 'tender spot' where self is inflamed, will differ with the individual, but the dying process may be as radical as it was with Jacob and leave us in some tangible way marked for life. But die we must.

The biblical exposition
In the lives of several biblical characters this principle
is depicted. Take Isaiah as an example. Is it not signifi-
cant that when he saw the glory of the Lord he was
immediately aware of the uncleanness of his own lips?
Probably Isaiah was one of the most 'golden-mouthed'
of the prophets, if his writings are any indication of his
ability. Right there, then, in the place that was a flourishing seed-plot for self-confidence and pride—right there,
he must die. If, as someone has remarked, we have no
right to touch the Lord's children with hands not yet
bearing the marks of the cross, what shall it be said of
lips that are to be the vehicle of His holy Word?

Space fails to tell of prophets such as Joshua, Daniel
and others whose encounter with God is recorded in
some detail and in every case brought with it such a
keen sense of unworthiness and absolute death of hope
in self, that only a touch from the Lord Himself brings
restoration and commission. They are literally raised up
to serve Him.

Let us finally turn to Paul as one who most clearly
has shown us the outworking of this principle in daily
victory and in respect to a truly Spirit-filled ministry.
The experience of the death to self finds several phases
in the experience of Paul. The most basic of them all
seems to be described in Galatians 2:20, where he speaks
of being crucified with Christ. He exhorts the same experience upon the Roman Christians in Romans 6:6,
saying that what has been established as an historical
fact, they have to make their own in active experimental
faith.

Galatians 2:20 is so vital to a balanced Christian life
and is so succinct an explanation of the secret of Paul's
undoubted power that we do well to take it as a key for
further discussion. Few have analysed it more cogently
than Norman Grubb at a series of addresses to missionaries in Japan in 1954. He pointed out how Paul oscil-
lates in this marvellous piece of spiritual psychology:

I'm crucified with Christ—no, no, I'm here—no, no, I'm not here, Christ lives in me—no, no, I live—no, no, I live by the faith of the Son of God—and that's the best that human language can do.

He went on to say:

If Christ lives in me, He lives His own life in me. We naturally seek abstractions like light, or power, or meekness, or faith, but though these abstractions are thus delineated for our understanding, faith is really a person believing and love is a person loving. He does not impart love to me; He loves in me, the loving Person inside me! He is the believing Person inside me.

No more need we moan for lack of faith. Rather, we need to lament our persistent confidence in our *own* ability or striving to believe. Reference could be made to Scriptures which point out how the Lord is Himself 'walking in' us, and 'working in' us, 'speaking in' us (not just to us or through us) and finally, He Himself is powerful 'in us'. He does not make *me* powerful! He Himself 'is powerful in you' is the biblical expression (2 Cor. 13:3). The problem in any lesser experience seems to lie in our failure to recognise and abide in this union constantly, and at the same time the tendency to move out of the union and to act independently.

Self is never obliterated. We never become a cipher or vacuum, but 'life is a liberated Christ inside a liberated personality'. The death, then, is the death of the independent self and all its unholy offspring, but it is a death that is desired by none of us till there is an adequate exposure of the independent self in all its earthiness and no-goodness.

The cameo of this in Galatians, the analysis of the divine-human relationship, is the 'I' of the independent Paul, as crucified with Christ. The 'I' of the dependent self lives, but it is not really 'I' at all but Christ living in him, and thus he is not a full man till he is a dependent man and lives by an imparted faith. We do not get to this by *trying* to be crucified; we *are* crucified! We accept this by faith and expect the Lord to make it real in our daily lives in successive unfoldings of His purposes as we are able to appropriate it. In the language of Romans 6:11, we consider ourselves dead, which for some has meant a real crisis of dramatic proportions. For us all, it is something we need to 'keep on reckoning'—as the Greek of verse 11 would imply. Self seems to have infinite resources for making an Agag-like plea for life and we can be as happy in a self-full religion as in grovelling sensuality, as long as self is independent. But once committed in totality to all that it means to be crucified with Christ, we can expect the Lord in all faithfulness and with infinite gentleness to lead us step by step in the outworking of that relationship in every aspect of life—till 'another opportunity to die' will not be shunned but accepted as from His own hand for our good and a richer experience of His resurrection power.

Dying to help others die
To Paul, the ministry of correction was no light affair. In 2 Corinthians 12:20, 21 there is quite an extraordinary sequence. Paul was fearful that the church was living up to its reputation of party jealousy and strife. He knew from experience that if he was to be the instrument of rebuke and correction when he arrived, it would mean personal humiliation for him also. But why? Why should God humble Paul before those He sends him to correct? He was not the cause of their strife. No, but apparently in the divine strategy, peace is made only by the peace-maker himself suffering much of the cost of reconciliation. To rebuke another helpfully, it is often necessary for us first of all to expose our own weakness and show the way the Lord has applied the cross to that particular problem in our lives; for no temptation comes to us but what is common to all—if we are honest

enough to admit it. This is never easy, for we much prefer that people think well of us. Whether there is a pulpit to stand in or not, we much prefer to talk down to others. But the cross spells certain death to sham, to hypocrisy, to all that is mere appearance, and only from the vantage-ground of utter reality and death to self-aggrandisement can we minister life to others.

A. J. Dain, in an article on Christian missions in a changing world, once said: 'For the mature missionary who is sent to the field, one characteristic is essential: humility. And the way to humility is death to self.' The true leader will excel in humility—that skin-tight garment the wearer is not conscious of but which is manifest enough to others. In the words of a Japanese proverb, the rice with the most grains in the ear bows closest to the ground.

In Romans 10 Paul declares himself willing to be accursed from God for His people's sake. Moses pleads for a similar identification with his people when, because of their return to idolatry, he asked to be blotted out of the book of life unless they could be forgiven (Exod. 32:32). The leader's consciousness of sin in another calls, therefore, not just for a stern word, seasonal though it may be, but for an identification with the needy one that results in costly intercession and sharing. The horror and shame of another's sin burns into his own heart as though the act of sin had been his very own.

Anyone, therefore, who becomes negatively critical of the people among whom he labours has already lost touch. His capacity to minister to them has probably already disappeared, whether he knows it or not. The seed yet abides alone.

Taking criticism to the cross
It is difficult enough to give correction in the spirit of humility, but even more difficult to take it from another in the same spirit. If a Christian is keen enough, there

will be friction somewhere. Through loose-tongued talk which inevitably occurs, hearsay may spring from appearances and give birth to deep-seated prejudice against him. From then on, no matter what he does, people look at his actions with a jaundiced eye. The more gifted he is, the more he will occasion envy, or his very oneness with the people to whom he ministers can produce sour grapes in the hearts of those who will not pay a similar cost of identification. He will be sorely tried by those who, refusing to walk in the light of Matthew 18 : 15, do not come to him for an explanation for things that trouble their consciences. The usual reaction is to speak out in self-defence among those with whom there is a natural affinity, and thus to deepen the rift in the whole fellowship. He may be more guarded and keep things to himself, but at the same time develop quite a huff, and determine that the critical can stew in the juice of their own prejudice. This may be the natural course, but it is sheer loss all round—to the critical and the criticised alike. The answer is the way of the cross—death to self-vindication and a simple obedience to the Scriptures which leave no room but for the criticised himself to take the initiative in self-humbling and go to the critical in person.

I recall personal reaction to criticism that was given to me in all honesty for my good, but which at the time I felt to be absurdly petty and unfounded. I went to pray about the matter, but I confess that it was with some heat of spirit. I found myself reading in Amy Carmichael's booklet *If* : 'If I feel injured when another lays to my charge things that I know not, forgetting that my Sinless Saviour trod this path to the end, then I know nothing of Calvary love.'

Now that should have been enough to bring me to my senses, but the next sentence reads : 'If I feel bitterly towards those who condemn me, as it seems to me, unjustly, forgetting that if they knew me as I know myself, they would condemn me much more, then I know nothing of Calvary love.'[1] Self-vindication, on that occasion at least, was brought to a justifiable and sudden death.

As responsible Christians, if our lives are going to demand the cross as their only sufficient explanation, it should not be surprising if, like Paul, we find that we 'die daily'.

1. Amy W. Carmichael, *If* (S.P.C.K.), pp. 38–9.

9

The Life of Faith

On three occasions the New Testament takes up the prophecy of Habakkuk 2:4, 'The righteous shall live by his faith', to give different slants to the life of faith. In Hebrews 10:38 the stress is on the need of persistent faith, in Galatians 3:11 on the necessity of faith alone apart from the law, and then in Romans 1:17 we are told that he who lives by faith thereby demonstrates the righteousness of God.

Hebrews 10:38, 39 comes as an introduction to the magnificent catalogue of the faithful in chapter 11, where men and women who have faith 'keep their souls', or who through faith and patience 'inherit the promises' (6:12). Whether it was Abel making an acceptable offering to God, or Enoch just walking with God and walking right into His presence; whether it was Abraham offering up his son in an act of obedient faith, or whether it was again Abraham just sojourning in the land of promise by faith; whether in crisis, therefore, or just in uneventful continuance, they lived by faith (11:5–17).

Today we tend to place great stress on the initial act of faith in some crisis experience that supposedly winds up the clock of a new spiritual life that should go on till we enter heaven. In actual fact, it is just the first of innumerable acts of faith in a growing experience of utter dependence upon God's faithfulness.

Further, the expression 'to live by faith' has in some circles come to mean a certain rather adventurous attitude that applies exclusively to missionaries and perhaps to some unusual workers at home, who receive no settled income and who take a special delight in being financially independent. On the contrary, it is my privilege to know Christians in business, for example, who have trusted the Lord to work in extraordinary ways to meet their need of suitable housing. One could itemise the incidents of simple faith that obviously had something to do with finding lost articles, finding one's way, regaining health, finding one's wits in the exam room, and finding a suitable partner for life!

Hudson Taylor was the founder under God of a missionary society which had some hundreds of missionaries. Though at the beginning he passed the place of no return as regards his simple trust in God's faithfulness to supply the needs of them all, in later years he still had to learn lessons of a daily rest of faith that simply transformed his subsequent ministry.[1]

Venturesome faith
Abraham had a solid promise that God was going to make him father of many nations. This promise, it would appear, was given deliberately when there was no human possibility of it being fulfilled, so that Abraham was 'constantly anticipating the birth of things that gave as yet no token of their existence'.[2] It will be remembered, however, that Abraham did have his times of doubt and sought to exploit other physical avenues to help God fulfil His impossible promises! But God shut him up to the impossible.

Isaac was not the last miracle 'child' by any means. We have known the Lord to give assurance that He would provide a worker for a specific need when humanly speaking there was no possibility of that person being available. We have proved that it is wiser not to try to pull strings or lobby with the best of intentions. We have only quietly to remind the Lord day by day of His own promises and see Him arrange circumstances to make the right person available.

My wife and I both independently came to have a special burden for a college in the city. Every time we passed it we had a strange compelling urge to see a Christian group established there. Initially this concern was given to us separately without the other knowing it was there. Humanly speaking, the chance of a Bible-believing group of students functioning in this place was impossible, yet the day did come when through the conversion of one and another, and the sympathy of a solitary evangelical professor, Christian students were able to arrange evangelistic meetings and now meet weekly on campus. It would appear that God challenges us to believe the impossible, and in obedience we have to venture out upon the fact of His having spoken.

If we put inner assurance over against the plainly written Word of God, then the venture is doomed from the start. I recall some discussion at a student conference when a professing Christian argued strongly for marriage with a non-Christian, 'as long as you had assurance', he said. I replied to the effect that I questioned the source of any assurance that was contrary to explicit passages in the Bible on the subject. The Holy Spirit never prompts us to do something that is plainly contrary to the Bible of which He is the Author.

I realise, however, that there are occasions when we are prompted to do a thing in circumstances where there is no specific biblical precedent, and in some cases where there is no sensible accompanying reason at the time. An example of this can be found in the story of David Wilkerson's first acceptable contact with the teenage gangs in New York.[3] The constraint to do something practical to help teenage youths accused of murder was unmistakable. His first attempt to help seemed to be quite disastrous; yet it proved that what appeared a ludicrous but well-meant bungle was the very thing that opened the door to a most effective redemptive ministry among them. The Lord does not necessarily explain why He asks us to do things a certain way, but later we are able to appreciate the wisdom of the venture when we see its effects.

Moses is a good example of this. Though often frustrated by the apparent failure of his mission to bring release to Israel, and although every judgment on the many gods of the Egyptians only brought further reprisals upon his complaining people, yet that same competition of plagues was a must if idolatry was to be thoroughly discredited in the eyes of the future dwellers in Canaan. Further, Moses naturally demurred at the possibility of failure, but apart from some initial signs accompanying his call, the Lord would only promise him that one day he would serve Him on the very mountain from which he was being sent (Exod. 3:10–12). In other words, the final proof that God had indeed sent him would come only after the venture of faith or obedience (the Old Testament word for faith) was consummated. We would like some indubitable evidence of ultimate success before we push off into the unknown or, like Jonah, we have our own conceptions of what that success will mean, and then get disheartened perhaps when the Ninevites are not destroyed!

If there were no venture to faith there would be little place for the exercise of faith at all. If the challenge were merely to meet some known and not too irksome duty, then we would merely adjust our schedule to suit. Time and again, however, the Lord challenges us to attempt what seems to us to be impossible. In faith we have to command some sun to stand still, some sea to open before His escaping people, or some devil of unbelief to depart from a distracted heart. We do so, not in some childish fantasy, but out of the stern necessity in the situation—some moral ultimatum that we perhaps dimly feel we share with the Lord Himself and we are merely executors of the will He has permitted us to see. Faith in this kind of situation is spontaneous—and almost automatic, for we know we are treading the path of obedience.

The more sensitive we are to the will of the Lord in this our generation, no doubt the more experiences we will have of this kind of faith life, for it appears that the Lord Himself is shut up to working through the faith of His servants even though it is He who Himself gives us the faith to believe what He is going to do, as well as the strength to fulfil our part in its execution.

Presumptuous faith
Faith is mere presumption, however, if we challenge the powers of darkness, or make claims as to things 'shortly to come to pass' when we have no word from God to that end. If we read the life of George Müller and are stirred to commence an orphanage like his on the basis of moving men to give through God by prayer alone, but have no clear word from God to that end, we may find ourselves with some hungry mouths to feed and not even a stamp for them to lick!

The Lord is not compelled to reproduce His George Müllers. To every man is given a measure of faith—his own measure (Romans 12:3). For one aspiring missionary seeking training it may mean stepping out into a seeming void because there is no human expedient or means by which the need can be met. To another there may be faith enough to believe that the Lord is going to supply work enough to pay for tuition at the Bible college he wishes to attend, and his faith can be just as real as that of the other. For myself, the latter course proved to be the Lord's will for me. In the process of having to work on days off, not only did my health benefit from the exercise, but friends were made who have been faithful to me all through the years of missionary life. Not till I left Bible college, so broke that I sold my bicycle to pay travelling expenses home, was I faced with the challenge to engage in some Christian work when I did not even have the money to pay the required fee. In this particular service the workers paid their own expenses. I was challenged to go, nevertheless, and, to my amazement, two gifts were handed to me during that time by people who were quite ignorant of my financial needs, gifts that, together, exactly made up my required fees! Frankly I had not gone expecting any miraculous deliverance, and was reluctant to go if it meant being a burden to others. But there was a 'must' in my bones and not a little encouragement from the mission leader. It is in the path of obedience that we see the miracle of His provision.

There is, of course, the danger that we either misinterpret our inner urges, giving them the authority of a 'Thus says the Lord' or mistakenly take isolated Bible passages that seem to suit some specific need. A missionary believed that the Lord would heal his sick child without recourse to available medical care. He believed. He prayed. The child died in his arms. Why? Had he previously experienced the Lord's touch with sickness less terminal than this, or heard of others who had been miraculously healed and thus expected a repetition? Or was he just ashamed to appear to be without faith because of his association with others who believed in healing by faith alone?

What makes it more complex is that Christians have been known to pray for the sick out of simple obedience to the command in James 5:14–16 and with no real assurance that the person would get better. The sick person also has not been in a condition to act responsibly with faith, and yet there has been sudden and complete healing—to the amazement of both the prayers and the healed alike. In one case if any attendant faith was necessary obviously it was with the friend of the sick person who requested that the prayer for the sick be made.

There are several unknown factors in situations like these but one of the more common mistakes is surely to presume that the Lord will 'do it again'. I well remember the publicity and excitement over the move to add fifty new members in one year to the missionary volunteer fellowship in the universities with which I was associated. By the end of the year fifty had actually signed; fifty-one in fact, but we later discovered that one had dropped out so that the number 'the Lord had given' was exactly fulfilled in answer to prayer and growing enthusiasm. Whereupon the mission secretary challenged students again to declare themselves as believing for a further fifty in the ensuing year, with most unhappy and embarrassing results. If the first venture was a God-inspired faith, then the second was probably not without some exhibitionism. The prize exhibit would have been the adventurous faith of the organisers. When the Holy Spirit leads us into some venture of faith, the end result is rather the quiet and unobtrusive way in which the Lord proves that He Himself has been both the Author and the Perfecter of the whole thing. There is an accompanying sense of rest and certitude that leaves no room for panic, and certainly no room for self-glory.

With the meeting of any need it is obvious that faith never becomes a mere matter of rote, a simple mastering of some special technique, or a combination that unfailingly unlocks the vault of great treasure. We are far too limited in our knowledge of the possible fruit of our importunity to dictate how best the Lord should answer—and when.

David must have been strongly tempted to assail the Philistines at Rephaim exactly as he had done with such recent success at Baal-perazim (2 Sam. 5:17–25). Fortunately he realised that guidance for yesterday is not guidance for today, and he again sought the Lord for express direction. As it happened, he was given entirely different tactics. We cannot afford to presume the validity of yesterday's deliverance in the face of today's needs. If we do, then gradually we get away from the Lord of Hosts and His hosts of ways of doing things, and trust in an empirical method, the machinery of His designing, instead of in the Designer Himself.

Missionaries in particular tend to suffer from the presumption that God can use them only in ways consistent with their experience in their own country. If they are not free enough in His hands, to welcome the unpredictable and rejoice in a ministry that would perhaps be inconsequential or insignificant at home, but is essential to the growth of a stable work abroad, then they will suffer the disillusionment that characterises too many who think they are not wanted and their gifts despised.

The life of faith among other things, therefore, expresses itself moment by moment in an anticipation of the Lord's capacity to do all *He* wants to do through us and, if necessary, in ways that we have never before experienced nor can we even visualise. We live 'in the holy carelessness of the eternal now', as George Macdonald said.

Corporate faith
To live by faith personally is one thing, but to experience positive acts of faith as a group can be quite different and a much more complex exercise.

Jesus said, 'If two of you agree on earth about anything they ask, it will be done for them . . .' (Matt. 18 : 19). Why the need of one more to add weight to the petition? Is the fact of two people agreeing about something sufficient to give it special unction in God's presence? Jesus goes on in verse 20 to speak about being in the midst of the twos and threes. Is the faith of the group, therefore, of more value than that of the individual Christian? It may not be of any more value in itself, but it will probably be more balanced and better informed. Possibly the important thing in the first place is whether or not we really do agree about something on earth.

According to John Wesley, the Bible has nothing to say about a solitary religion. It is safe to say that in Paul's ministry and missionary strategy there is little evidence of solitary missionaries. We desperately need each other. The Christian who likes to be a lone wolf is apt to be dangerous, not only to others, but also to himself. I have seen missionaries become independent out of mere petulance, because their pet schemes are not accepted. They do not care to submit their ideas to the bar of prayerful public opinion, and more often than not they feel that no one else has a right to question how they use 'the Lord's money'. They feel that that particular area is sacred—to themselves, that is!

In three places in the Proverbs of Solomon it is asserted that there is wisdom in having a number of counsellors. It is possible, of course, for a group of Christians to be spiritually dull, and only one—presumably the leader—to be sensitive to the Lord's will. However, even in such a situation the wise leader will refrain from taking action over their heads, and refuse to move till the others with good heart are able to move with him. This can call for much prayerful patience. The leader needs to believe that if some step is of God, then He is able to make the rest of the fellowship see it in His own time. His personal faith in a certain line of action must become a corporate one if it is to be carried to any good effect.

Some leaders rather proudly claim that they are not 'committee men', and will joke about the best committee being one in which the secretary is sick and the treasurer is out of town; but this can often be a mere confession of smallness of mind. If our essential ministry was just to produce spiritual children, with no thought of their subsequent growth into maturity, the claim would be valid. Neither Jesus nor Paul worked on that assumption. They deliberately surrounded themselves with others who greatly needed the inspiration and example of their leadership. They lived a kind of perpetual committee life!

The Lord's mind is not always revealed to us directly, nor when we meet together about some problem is it always revealed to the most vociferous, nor through a chairman with particularly acute powers of analysis or uncanny capacity for pleasing everyone at the same time. On a number of occasions, both at home and abroad, I have had the experience of seeing a student committee or missionary group about to take action along a certain line, when perhaps, the quietest member among us has had the courage to disagree, and offer an entirely different, and perhaps contrary, solution to the problem. Upon further reflection this was gladly accepted by all, and it later proved to be the Lord's 'still small voice'.

If the leader has the assurance that group experiences of finding the Lord's will is the biblical norm—as a number of scriptures would indicate—then he can approach meetings in faith, believing that lasting results will not just depend upon the strength of his own leadership, but upon his believing—indeed, the whole group believing with him—that in some way the Lord is going to speak to them all. To approach executive meetings, therefore, with one's mind made up, or with the kind of prejudice that will grieve the Holy Spirit in the midst, or with much heat of spirit and therefore very little light, is to spell doom from the start. This, of course, does not mean that the leader should come to a meeting unprepared and without the facts of each case at his finger tips. 'Facts are the fingers of God,' said A. T. Pierson. However, some major problems appear insoluble because facts of equal importance seem to mount up on both sides of the question in conflicting array, and only a prayerful act of united faith will produce the key to a forward move.

It is in open-hearted fellowship with others who are

also anxious to know the mind of the Lord that one
realises, with the saintly Rutherford, that 'our aspirations are not canonical'. Even when we are most convinced that we are doing God's will, at the back of our
minds we need to consider the possibility of having
been mistaken.

Faith is based upon some word from God. We can
claim only what He has promised. Faith is not whipped
up in our hearts by the stimulus of united prayer and
much hymn-singing—not true faith, that is. We need a
measure of inspiration in these ways, it is true, but
group faith, to be healthy, needs to be based upon some
clear word from the Lord Himself—the kind from which
we cannot escape. A student group may seem about to
fade out through lack of effective leadership; a missionary family may be in desperate and unforeseen financial straits; a local church may be facing some moral
crisis which calls for precipitate action; young missionaries or national workers may be facing the fearful unknown of a new assignment; these and like situations
call for a word from the Lord Himself, and with it the
whole group can come to a deep sense of the rightness
of things that is a source of immeasurable strength to
any one individual concerned.

Faith's trials
According to James, the trial of faith is necessary, for
it flexes the muscles of faith and encourages healthy
growth (Jas. 1:3, 4). This we may agree to in principle
and still be very surprised at the nature and duration
of the tests that do come our way. Like Abraham, we
may be challenged to a test of allegiance and priorities
in affection that seem to negate the very promise we
have previously received from Him. We may feel the
demand is unreasonable and utterly impossible to perform. But He does not command the impossible. He
may seem to on occasion, but it is only to throw us more
upon His own resources, that we may prove, in fact,

that it is indeed He who is 'at work in you, both to will and to work for his good pleasure' (Phil. 2:13). In many cases the greatest battle lies in the willingness to *attempt* the apparently impossible. Abraham had to raise the knife before the alternate sacrifice was given. The man with the palsied hand had to stretch it out before it was made whole (Mark 3:5). We must act just because He commands it, not because we think that we can do it.

There may be some clear promise from the Lord and yet it never seems to see fulfilment—certainly not in the way we expect. Perhaps this was one of the reasons for John the Baptist's queries as to the Lord's Messiahship (Matt. 11:2–6), for there seemed little sign of the 'unquenchable fire' that John expected. His, therefore, was the problem of rightly interpreting the Lord's mind and ministry. Perhaps he was puzzled, too, at being incarcerated for his faithfulness. But he did the wise thing —took his problem to the Lord and received that steadying answer that has upheld many a perplexed Christian of subsequent times, 'Blessed is he who takes no offence at me' (Luke 7:23).

Habakkuk's trial of faith was somewhat similar, for he obviously found it difficult to understand just how the Lord could permit His own people to be a doormat for a heathen nation to walk on, a nation more sinful than his own. In the face of the incomprehensible, his faith soared to the place where he could say 'Though the fig tree do not blossom, nor fruit be on the vines, the produce of the olive fail and the fields yield no food, the flock be cut off from the fold and there be no herd in the stalls, yet will I rejoice in the Lord, I will joy in the God of my salvation' (Hab. 3:17, 18). Circumstances will slander God again and again, yet it is in the very tensions of the unexplained and unexpected trial that we are called upon to demonstrate that we hold to the faithfulness of God. That is the invariable quantity. The revelation of His nature in Scripture makes it clear that He cannot contradict Himself.

Perhaps the most common test of faith for us all is when we set out in obedience to the Lord's command in some way, and then sooner or later meet with the most distressing opposition from all sides. One can only imagine what was in the heart of the disciples at finding themselves in the midst of the storm after being expressly ordered to the other side of the lake by the Lord Himself (Matt. 14:22). He, incidentally, had for the present stayed safely on shore. Then He came to them walking on the very waves that terrified them! No doubt this test was one of the things which transformed their 'little faith' into the stable faith that was neither surprised nor overwhelmed when the early Church was buffeted by the winds of opposition and the waves of disaster. Indeed, they seemed more surprised at the miraculous answer to prayer for Peter's deliverance from prison (Acts 12:15), than at the opposition following their fearless preaching of the Gospel. In the latter case they simply prayed for more boldness in preaching, and certainly not for protection (Acts 4:23–31). Their eyes were no longer on the wind and the waves but on the One whom they had proved was well able to carry through to completion His own purposes for them and through them.

I remember how, after commencing the building of our house here in Japan with amazingly appropriate promises from the Bible, and equally amazing gifts to help the project step by step as we proceeded, we found ourselves at the mercy of unscrupulous tradesmen and beset by all sorts of trials. Before its completion it caught fire and could have burnt to the ground but for the Lord's intervention. Had not the Lord commanded us? Could He not have prevented these things? What He did do was to prompt me to prepare a bath the night before the fire though we hadn't planned to have one. Japanese baths are deep and the water remained till next morning so there was ample available to extinguish the flames even though we live in a place where at that time no water was quickly obtainable. Without that water the house would have been a total loss, and with no insurance at that time! Actually, as a result of the fire, gifts were given that more than compensated for the damage and enabled us to proceed further with the completion of the building.

However, even though one can accept opposition and trial of this sort, what of the times when the Lord seems to fail? What of a missionary in Japan whose house was not only burned down but their child was burned to death as well? What of the wife who feels sure the Lord has answered her prayers for a child late in life only to have the pregnancy terminate in miscarriage with no further hope of children? What of the girl who prays much about a proposal for marriage from a keen Christian and feels definitely led to say yes, only to have him later break the engagement because he feels led to go abroad? What about a young graduate of a college of education who applies for a position believing that God has clearly led, and the position goes to a friend of lower teaching marks, because of the prejudice of one member of the Board, who happens to dislike the particular groups she worships with? What of the young Christian who is active in Christian work and full of promise for the future, but who is suddenly smitten with a disabling disease and is a cripple for the rest of his life? What of the young missionary who goes to the field after all the preparation involved, only to be invalided home after a few months?

Admittedly, in some of these cases known to the writer, there has later been a redirection into a life and ministry that probably is all the richer and more useful for the anguish of the unexplained. It is not what happens to us that can be so hurtful; it is what we do with what happens. The unexpected calamity can make us bitter and reproachful, or we can accept the whole experience in the light of the cross, saying 'Thy will be done'. It is this kind of faith that throws the tree into the bitter waters to make them sweet (Exod. 15:25) and, if we can carry the analogy a little further, it is from these waters that so many are refreshed.

One of the most challenging studies in the life of faith comes from the comparison of the inspiring list in Hebrews 11:32–5 of those who through faith had done extraordinary things and experienced amazing deliverances, with that in Hebrews 11:36–8 of those who suffered horrid mutilations and violent death. It is of the latter that the writer says the world was not worthy. They did not receive physical deliverance and yet never lost their faith. Among them there would have been those who had seen others delivered from the tormentor in quite a singular and miraculous way. Why not them too?

Relatives of missionaries who lost their lives in the Congo uprising would have occasion to ask the same question. Some missionaries were delivered from the Simbas in breathtaking, apparently miraculous escapes, and others (who had served the country and its people for decades and surely 'deserved' to live) were cut off by utterly irresponsible and youthful fanatics. Did John's disciples feel the same way when their revered leader was beheaded because of a foolish and regretted promise to an erotic dancer by a drunken king? Could the Lord not have prevented *that* disaster if after all, as He said Himself, John was the greatest of the prophets (Matt. 11:11)? Surely of all the people the Lord's own forerunner deserved a dignified finale to his faithful ministry. Yet it would appear that just how we terminate this life is of minor consideration; what matters is that we maintain an attitude of confidence in the Lord Himself and refuse to take offence at what the Lord permits in our lives. We may on occasion be left like John with but the faith of allegiance when we have lost the faith of assurance.

The incident described in Daniel 3 of the three Hebrew men in Babylonian captivity is very much to the point, for the integrity of their faith was more vital than the duration of their life or the manner of its termination. They felt sure that God could deliver them from the impending death by fire. But if, for some reason they could not see, the Lord did not intervene in this present occasion then they still would not compromise on the basic issue of idolatry. This was simple allegiance to the God they did know, and to the things they did know pleased Him, while they freely admitted that there were things about God's will for them that they could not know, and yet about which they could trust Him. One feels that the Lord was almost obliged to answer in some miraculous way a faith like that! Yet if they had perished in the fire, as others have done, to die in triumphant faith that God's ripest purposes were being fulfilled, would be every bit as wonderful as to be taken through the fire without hurt.

Faith, then, is not an insurance against trial, but an introduction to trial. It is not a tool we can use for physical deliverance or the supply of our needs without fail, but a pathway of obedience and a principle of action that keeps us from being the plaything of circumstances and the victim of changeable feelings. No wonder a tried and mature faith is so precious in the sight of God—more precious than silver or gold (1 Pet. 1:7).

1. See Dr and Mrs Howard Taylor, *Hudson Taylor's Spiritual Secret* (Overseas Missionary Fellowship), pp. 110–65.

2. Rom. 4:17, translated by Arthur S. Way in *Letters of Paul and Hebrews* (Macmillan).

3. See David Wilkerson, *The Cross and the Switchblade* (Lakeland Paperbacks), pp. 13–30.

10

Taking the Initiative

If we look back from the vantage-point of several years in the Christian life, it will appear from the distinct pattern now emerging that all our ways have been ordered by the Lord. He seems to have left nothing to chance. Even a temporary vacillation on our part does not seem greatly to have affected the general trend. We also recall, however, that at every time of crisis, and indeed in the humdrum of the every day, the whole issue of things seemed to depend entirely upon ourselves. At times we were left, it would appear, to a most unexciting and naked obedience. That we do ourselves have complete freedom to choose either the right path or the wrong one follows as a corollary from the fact that some day we are to be called into judgment as Christians for the deeds done in the body—a stewardship of time and talent that calls for some final accounting. Now, you don't judge an automaton. You don't send a robot to jail. In short, the initiative lies with us. Equally, the initiative lies with God.

It proves to be a most profitable study to go through the Bible noting the places where both the sovereignty of God and the freedom of the will of man are treated together. In some places the two themes are interwoven in the same incident. Take Luke 22:22 as an example.

Here Jesus is telling His disciples that He is going to His death 'as it has been determined', presumably by God Himself, and yet woe is invoked on the man by whom He is betrayed. Later on Peter in his first sermon after Pentecost courageously tells the wondering mob that Jesus was delivered to death by God's counsel (Acts 2:23). Yet they have wickedly slain Him and are therefore culpable.

J. I. Packer, in his book *Evangelism and the Sovereignty of God*, points out that God and man stand in such a relation to each other that they can both be free agents in the same action. He goes on to say that this antinomy, i.e. an observed relation between two sets of facts that is both unavoidable and insoluble, can be avoided only by falsifying the facts. Nature gives us an example in the two equally credible theories of light, one idea based on the fact of waves, and the other on the fact of particles, both with factual evidence, yet seemingly impossible the one to the other. 'Such a necessity scandalises our tidy minds, no doubt, but there is no help for it if we are to be loyal to the facts.'[1]

Turn to those mysterious and apparently contradictory remarks of the Lord in John 6:63–7. On the one hand, He tells us that the Spirit alone can give life. Jesus knows from the beginning who will not believe in Him; no one comes to Him unless it is the will of the Father. On the other hand, He turns to the disciples asking them if they also will follow the crowd who have been offended at these hard sayings. Did He not know, or was it just a rhetorical question? Apparently the others did have the freedom to reject the Lord's claims, and reject them they did. The disciples apparently did have the freedom to cleave to Him, and stay they did— though imperfectly.

Charles Simeon spoke of the truth of God's sovereignty and man's free will as being truth in two extremes, both equally true and to be held with equal tension so that one does not eclipse or modify the other.[2] Fusion of the two is beyond reason, and so we can only say with Paul, 'I exert all my strength in reliance upon the power of Him who is mightily at work in me' (Col. 1:29, Weymouth). At no time do we become a mere cipher and yet, mercifully, at no time are we left to fight it out alone.

The Israelites are led into a complete impasse leaving them with no alternative but either God's sovereign and miraculous intervention or a return to slavery. The initiative seems without doubt to be with Him, and yet is it? The sea is not divided before them till Moses lifts high his rod, thus in one act confirming his often-disputed leadership among them, and giving tangible evidence that God refuses to work His miracles apart from man taking the initiative that is rightly his. The whole church can pray without ceasing, as if on prayer alone hung the issue of the day, and yet only God can bring Peter out of prison, to the utter and touching bewilderment of those who would not believe in the answer to their own prayers! I depend, therefore, upon God alone. Yet at the same time God, in some sense at present beyond fine calculation, is depending upon me and 'waits' for me to take the initiative.

Let us now consider some ways in which the initiative does appear to lie solely with us and then in conclusion consider our task as leaders to train others to take the initiative in their own lives where they should.

Self-help

Most Christians, especially if converted in their teens, would probably confess to a tremendous stimulus through that experience to improve themselves in every way. The 'reformation' in this case is followed by a kind of renaissance. For myself, till converted at the age of eighteen I had been content to read little and dream much, but then the whole inner man seemed to be bathed with an unquenchable thirst for knowledge, so much so that labour at a trade during the day became burdensome for the longing to be home to my books in the evening. I then had to ask the Lord for an interest in my daily work because its evident lack had become a poor witness.

Later the way opened for university studies and, though far from being the stuff of which scholars are made, how grateful I am now for an incentive that put me on the stretch beyond natural powers. Otherwise I would still be wallowing in the slough of wishful thinking or mere envy of those more richly endowed.

A keen dissatisfaction with present achievement and knowledge should be the normal mark of a healthy Christian life. If this attitude is of God, then the implementing of it and most of the initiative as to how that urge bears fruit lies squarely with us, for otherwise we shall be found to quench the Holy Spirit within us.

We certainly cannot excuse ourselves simply on the grounds of lack of genius or natural gift. William Carey seemed to be genius enough, but he declared that all he had was the ability to plod, the capacity for taking pains. Few can rank with Leonardo da Vinci in his extraordinary contribution to the fields of painting, sculpture, architecture and science alike. But he prays, 'O Lord, Thou sellest to us all, gifts at the price of effort. Genius is defined by some as 10 per cent inspiration and 90 per cent perspiration. Livingstone, as a Christian lad of ten, bought a Latin grammar from his first week's wages and pursued his studies far into the night even though he had to be at work by 6 a.m. He apparently placed his books on the spinning jenny so that he could catch sentence after sentence as he passed in the course of his work. Little wonder that he did so well later in theology and medicine and became the bridgehead to modern missions in Africa. He later paid tribute to the necessity of such a hardy training and said he would be willing to endure it again, for the sake of all that it yielded.

Most of us are too easily satisfied; our goals are too low. We are happy just to pass when we probably have the capacity to excel. If, for example, we can make ourselves merely understood in a foreign language then we are satisfied, even if, like David Brainerd among the Indians, we find they understand 'my low and vulgar methods of expression because they were familiar with my voice'! We tire not because our minds are so tired but because we have lost interest. Like the rest of the body, given sufficient incentive the mind is capable of prodigious labours. A mere change of intellectual pursuit will soon reveal how elastic it really is.

The example of an aged missionary in Japan comes readily to mind. He was famous for his knowledge of idiomatic Japanese, yet (for the sake of the divinity students among whom he laboured) apparently worked till late in the evenings perfecting new ways of saying things in this incredibly rich language. I venture to say that his example must have stimulated the young and at the same time kept *him* young, for the brain seems to be one of the last of our organs to suffer the debilitating effects of age—provided that we refuse to let it die from sheer atrophy.

Initiative in the Christian is conditioned first of all by the fact that capacity for achievement in any field differs according to the individual. We are commanded not to think more highly of ourselves than we ought, and yet we are to do all things heartily as unto the Lord. The heart motive is the primary thing, but a Christian without ambition should be a contradiction in terms. It is a case of 'my utmost for His highest'.

Too many of us merely drift from weekend spiritual stimulus to stimulus, with perhaps a major 'shot in the arm' at the annual convention for the deepening of the spiritual life, but we are soon back in the rut again; a little more wistful perhaps but hardly less useless.

Paul's life, on the other hand, was characterised by clear-cut goals, some of which he attained. Even if he

never attained them all, his was a phenomenal achievement for the simple reason that his goals were so high.
Better to aim too high and partly achieve something than
to aim at nothing and reach that.

Paul determined to reach the world's metropolis with
the gospel, but probably did not expect to get there as
a guest of the imperial government! He was determined
to preach Christ where His name had not yet been heard,
and so he had a lot of elbow-room. The longest he stayed
in any one place seems to have been about two years.
He was determined by all means to win some to Christ,
and the 'all means' stretched all his ingenuity and his
massive intellectual powers to the utmost. He laboured
to see every convert mature in Christ, 'God labouring
in him mightily' to that end.

For ourselves, we might profitably consider a number
of fields in which some definite goals are needed.

Personal evangelism
Personal evangelism is a case in point. Moody determined to speak to at least one person a day about Christ,
even if, out of forgetfulness, he had to get out of bed at
night to do it! This may appear to some to be very artificial and almost to veto the leading of the Spirit, but it
was characteristic of the man that he did nothing by
halves for he was determined to be a man God could
use. No one method is the answer for us all, and the
person we seek to evangelise would be the first to detect
any artificial mimicry of men who are being specially
used.

Most of us swing from a vague wistfulness that we
might be used to win someone to the Saviour to the odd
occasions when we are really convicted of lack of concern and we feel we should do something definitely
about this business of personal evangelism. Rosalind
Rinker has made some valuable suggestions in connection with faith-sized requests in her book on prayer
that can well apply to this problem.[3]

Rather than pray vaguely to be used for the salvation of someone we know, she suggests that we pray for something that is a step to that end, but which is something tangible—a realisable target within the compass of our own faith. In the beginning, to use her illustration, it may be just for the opportunity to meet casually a neighbour on a particular day. Later, it may be to claim in faith the opportunity to ask them for a meal and then the opportunity of conversation about spiritual things and so on. Whatever the method, a definite goal of faith or endeavour calls for initiative on our part and will be fruitful of good.

Profitable reading
Reading is said to make a full man, and writing an exact man. To get the most out of our reading, some of us need a combination of the two, as we find that only as we write a summary of what we have read do we fully register what we have learnt. Most books are not worth the effort, but those that are worth mastering sometimes call for several consecutive readings. Many study the Bible with notebook and pencil in hand, for they feel they need a definite incentive to find something worth recording for the day. The more familiar we become with the Scripture text, the more we need to take initiative in the way of definite study goals each year, or we tend to drift into mere rote reading where nothing definite registers. I change my Bible-reading method each year to avoid a rut but no one method can suit us all, nor is any one method suitable for all the time.

We live in a 'digest' age. Great books are abbreviated to suit the breathlessness of our times, but the Bible yields its choicest jewels only to some patient digging. According to Sir Joshua Reynolds, there is no expedient to which a man will not resort to avoid the real labour of thinking. Dr A. W. Tozer, in an article on the proper use of our mental powers, once argued that most people's thinking is done for them by professionals. The rest of us think only in the most elementary way. He writes, 'By about twenty-five years of age, most of us have left off serious habits of observation, the basis of growing knowledge, and our powers begin to atrophy and the habits of life are formed. We accept the conventions, lose our sense of wonder, and settle down to live by our glands and appetites. After that, about all we observe is the weather and the football score!'

Learning in the simplest terms he declared to be based upon observation, cogitation and reading (plus, we might add, active recall). A child learns quickly because of his keen powers of observation and insatiable curiosity. In this regard I have often recalled the saying attributed to Augustine, that in the learning of foreign languages, free curiosity is of more value than frightful enforcement. The same could go for any kind of learning, of course.

Dr A. T. Pierson began his little classic *Godly Self Control* with the observation, 'As to the power to think, we know not what is most overwhelming, the grandeur of the ability or the awfulness of the responsibility.' He was a keen advocate of controlled observation and disciplined reading. He testified to the fact that the years of his greatest intellectual progress were when he confined himself to half a dozen first-class books. The Christian cannot afford to dissipate his mental powers on what is merely amusing, merely to while away his time.

Dedicated time

The Christian's time is not his own. We are expressly commanded to buy it back from the worthless or, as Weymouth has it, to buy up the opportunities and make time yield dividends (Eph. 5:16; Col. 4:5). This surely does not mean we are called upon to live in an atmosphere of rush, trying to do the impossible for God in the shortest possible time, and connoting feverish activity with God-directed service, and area with depth. It does call for definite planning, however, for as the Puritan theologian Jeremy Taylor said, 'The first element of a holy life is the control of time.' According to Oswald Chambers, a holiday is no mere interlude but is like a parenthesis in a sentence. The sentence goes on afterwards with deeper meaning.

The schedule for one will be quite unsuited to another. Some of us need more sleep than others. Some of us can cram into one hour, by dint of training and natural gift, what another will take hours to do. Some can skim through a book with incredible speed while another has to read every word or lose the sense of the whole. These differences are incidental to the main factor that each according to his own ability should stop drifting and take the initiative in planning that each day yield its dividends of progress and attainment in our maturing Christian life.

J. O. Sanders says in one of his books,

> The solemn thing about time is, of course, that it can be lost, and time lost can never be regained. It cannot be hoarded; it must be spent. It cannot be postponed; it is irretrievably lost. How supremely important then, that we make full use of the time allotted to us in the fulfilment of our life purpose.[4]

Time, therefore, and the latent capacity for diligent toil, are heritages into which the Christian is called upon to enter and for which he will be called into account, or he, like Esau, will miss the privileges of his birthright.

Training others to take initiative
While still inexperienced as leaders, we can and should begin to encourage others to do things we perhaps feel sure we can do better ourselves. It follows the methods of the most enviable Bible college one could imagine, namely the Lord and His disciples. He appears to have worked on the principle of concentric circles of widen-

ing influence and intimacy, beginning with Peter, James and John, who had special revelations of His person and work. The rest of the twelve on the outer fringe were perhaps less privileged but hardly less involved in this walk-about Bible school. There were other disciples also, though not chosen to 'be with Him', as Mark described it.

The nature of the Lord's training methods are not immediately obvious in much detail but it does appear that He did nothing for the disciples that they could do for themselves. Though doing as much as possible with them, He did nothing instead of them, except wash their tired and dusty feet as a well-earned rebuke!

They were not mere tools of His self-realisation, but in seeking to reproduce Himself in them, He aimed at their individual maturity.

With Paul, we see the same principle written large, for though in gifts and initiative he towered head and shoulders above his contemporaries, he still deliberately chose to work with others who in the main seemed to have been younger than himself, some of them his own converts, and then farmed them out to positions of grave responsibility. Today's Christian leader can similarly gauge his success by the measure in which he has been used to train others to take initiative, and to do things in the energy of the Spirit when he himself is not around either to stimulate or to restrain. We can duplicate ourselves not by virtue of assuming more and more responsibilities but by encouraging others to tackle tasks beyond their present strength and wisdom (to our way of thinking) while we wait for them to make the inevitable mistakes which, incidentally, is just the way we have learnt most of what we happen to know.

Most of us do not take instinctively to this kind of training ministry, any more than the average father seems to have the patience to stand by his growing child in each tiny crisis with an 'I'll do it this once more for you, and then I'm sure you can do it yourself from now on. You try.' No, we haven't the time. We want the satisfaction of the job well done (we think) and done soon, because we think more of our valuable time and the exercise of our special gifts than of the more patience-consuming policy of helping others to grow up. Some of us are just too selfish and possessive and act towards younger believers like a senile principal of a kindergarten determined to keep the 'dear little children' as dear and as little as long as possible.

On the other hand some, and missionaries in particular, expect too much from young Christians. We single out the keen ones before others with words of praise or for positions of responsibility, and thus often engender pride and a major spiritual collapse. Again and again I have seen nationals chosen by foreigners as congenial fellow-workers, because of their foreign-like ways, but who for the same reason were suspect to their own people! With the Oriental, decisions can too easily be made just to please the persistent foreigner, and I have myself been too easily attracted to some open-hearted seeker who seems to have literally tumbled into the kingdom but whose staying power is nil when it comes to facing the offence of the cross.

Paul's command to Timothy to entrust the truth to faithful men who could teach others also (2 Tim. 2:2) was no mean command. He was both young and a foreigner. He had to be warned not to lay hands of ordination on any man suddenly, for it is a characteristic of youth to be easily impressed by zeal rather than by quiet steadfastness. No doubt faithfulness in his day carried overtones of suffering for Jesus's sake, but the choice of such future leaders for the local church or churches of which he was the bishop was one of his major ministries. Similarly, with us the preparation of leaders for service must never become just an adjunct to preaching the gospel, nor something that others might do but for which we have neither the time nor the inclination. For it is an integral part of our ministry from the beginning. Every new convert is for that very reason a potential leader in some capacity or other. It is our business to see that all his latent talents are developed to the uttermost.

Teaching methods
While teaching in a seminary soon after my arrival in Japan, I set some assignment papers in complete ignorance of current teaching and examination methods in this land. A student came to me soon afterwards greatly distressed because she could not find the answer to some of the questions in the notes I had given previously. I was equally astonished that it did not occur to her that I was expecting her to find the answer herself as a result of private study. I have seen since that a whole culture can be against the ordinary person coming to a private judgment from personal study. In Japan at that time the teacher was expected to have definite ideas, but not the rank and file. It was sufficient for the student to sit at his preceptor's feet and repeat him verbatim as the occasion served. This seemed to be the feudalistic concept of the teacher-student relationship that then prevailed in varying measure.

In a situation like this, I have seen students sit through a profoundly moving and overwhelmingly logical message apparently completely untouched. Upon questioning there seemed to have been no inclination to apply the import of the words to themselves. On the other hand, the reverence for some special teacher can be such that there is a blind obedience to his every wish. The latter state of affairs can be quite satisfying for the missionary if he is not careful, for it serves to make him feel indispensable, till he wakes up to realise that he is merely dangling robots on the strings of his fallible opinion.

In our work in Japan we have therefore sought to encourage Christians to be more dependent upon the Holy Spirit, to help them find the Lord's perfect will through the Word alone. In Bible study groups we have prepared questions from the passage under consideration that serve to bring out the writer's apparent meaning, and the students have answered the questions without hint or prompting. One group soon caught on to this method and then prepared the questions themselves. The first night this took place my wife and I also prepared questions on the passage in case the students did not rise to the occasion, but were greatly encouraged, even if somewhat embarrassed, when they turned up with questions that were much more interesting and pertinent to the needs of the students present than ours!

The same principle needs to be borne in mind when dealing with the problems of young Christians personally. I recall being visited by a Christian who was still young in faith and who was soon to return from university for his summer vacation to his home town. He was an only son and his mother apparently a very capable and domineering business woman. She was also an ardent Buddhist and the son knew that she would expect him to observe the usual family ritual at the shrine of his departed father. He loved his mother and had no desire either to cause her pain or create a scene, and besides he was of a very timid disposition. He asked me if it would not be permissible, under the circumstances, merely to give lip reverence to the family altar and, while bowing before it, in his heart to worship the true God whom he had come to know.

My reply, if I recall aright, was based first of all upon the moral obligation he had to his unsaved mother and then I appealed to him from the experience of others who had been faithful in like circumstances and also no doubt gave him some Bible verses to encourage him. Later, after rethinking in prayer what I had said, it occurred to me very forcibly that the thing that would remain uppermost in his mind would no doubt be my opinion of what he should do—just that, and little more. That being the case, he was very likely to think that I, being a foreigner, probably did not understand how difficult it is to brush aside these centuries-old customs, and so he would do what others have done: go to a Japanese friend or pastor hoping for a softer answer. What I should have done was first of all point him to some passage or passages of the Bible that obviously were applicable to this situation and, after getting him to read them, ask just what the Lord was saying to him through them.

Too often we presume to think that the Bible alone is just not quite enough, that it needs our experience to back it up; or, more often than not, the Bible is an adjunct to our experience and just happens to confirm what we have proved to be true. Paul's injunction to the young Timothy is not without point here; he was to preach the *Word* (2 Tim. 4:2). I still fail when caught off guard, but aspire more and more to using the Word and encouraging the youngest Christian to see that the Word itself has a sufficient answer to any problem he faces; that he should primarily be dependent upon the Holy Spirit to lead him and not be subject to the variable opinions of Christian friends alone. We can encourage him in this personal obedience to the Scriptures in large measure by the way we teach.

David Bentley-Taylor in *The Weathercock's Reward* has a section on the matter of training others that will serve to conclude this study. He speaks of Kraemer's survey of work among the Javanese where he found they were not ready for independence.

> In most churches they were far from being self-supporting, scarcely capable of being self-governing, and at best making tentative efforts at self-propagation. Furthermore there reigned among the Javanese Christians an overwhelming sense of their own weakness. And for these short-comings Kraemer felt that the missionaries were partly to blame. They had laboured hard among the Javanese

and had declared their intention to make themselves unnecessary. But, in actual practice, the conviction that they were absolutely indispensable had become deeply rooted in Javanese hearts. Their work had been *for the Javanese* rather than *through the Javanese*. Instead of having worked themselves out of a job, they were in greater demand than ever, and he found the Mission did not yet seem to possess the key which would unlock the hidden sources of power in the Javanese soul. Foreigners were generally so conscious of the deficiencies of the Javanese character, that deep in their hearts they did not really believe that the churches could function independently, and therefore they did not work with utter determination to achieve it.[5]

The interesting thing is that the measure in which we have had to stretch personal initiative to the full to gain any education or experience we may have does not mean we will automatically encourage others to exploit the same personal resources for themselves or their churches. With some it can work in inverse proportion. The diligence and discipline required through the years can make us impatient with the slothful and poorly endowed. It becomes a matter of principle that things must be done well and soon, regardless of who does them. So we do them ourselves!

We need to join again the training of the Twelve and then do a graduate course with Paul, till like Timothy we will not only be able to fulfil our own God-given ministry, but be wise enough to 'appoint elders in every town'.

1. J. I. Packer, *Evangelism and the Sovereignty of God* (Inter-Varsity Press), chapter 2.

2. See Handley Moule, *Charles Simeon* (Inter-Varsity Press), pp. 77–81.

3. See Rosalind Rinker, *Prayer: Conversing with God* (Zondervan), pp. 68–73.

4. J. O. Sanders, *Problems of Christian Discipleship* (Lutterworth), p. 119.

5. David Bentley-Taylor, *The Weathercock's Reward* (Overseas Missionary Fellowship), p. 98.

II

Discerning the Body

This expression comes from 1 Corinthians 11:29 and is part of Paul's rebuke of certain believers who, in their mere thoughtlessness at the Lord's supper, were displaying a sad lack of understanding of the nature of the Church.

For most of us as pastors or missionaries, our main concern is with the unity of the local church or churches where we are ministering, but the part of the local church in the nation-wide or world Church is a consideration we all must face in varying degrees. For this reason, we must first seriously consider the aims of the ecumenical movement in relation to the world Church, seeking to discern the measure in which this is truly a biblical expression of the Body of Christ.

The World Church
There are probably very few missionaries even in remoter areas of pioneer evangelism who are not under pressure to some extent these days from the ecumenical movement. Further, thinking students even in countries that are strongly Buddhist as in Japan, where Christianity is a pitiful minority in society, will ask repeatedly why it is that if Christianity is supposed to be the only true religion, there are so many sects 'warring against

each other'. Is the thought of one uniform world-wide Church the only consistent answer to that question? Leaders in the ecumenical movement would say a decided 'yes'.

However, a great body of opinion in the Church would say that the whole effort at ecclesiastical uniformity is an unwitting admission of spiritual bankruptcy. Malcolm Muggeridge reacted with trenchant criticism in an interview discussing this subject by suggesting that it all reminded him of when he was a boy watching the pubs turn out at night. He had a vivid memory of about twenty people, all very drunk, reeling out of the pub's doors, and they all had their arms around each other's shoulders, because if they didn't they would fall down. 'That to me, is a perfect picture of ecumenism,' he said. Certainly a study of the statistics of faltering church growth in denominations connected with the ecumenical movement would support this rather bizarre illustration.

An equally sad feature of the modern movement is the lack of tolerance towards those who refuse to conform. On the other hand there is tolerance of the strangest members within its ranks to the place where one wonders just how far they are willing to go to present a façade of apparent unity. To them, doctrine divides, but to put 'unity' before purity of doctrine is ultimately to destroy the basis of any real fellowship in the Spirit. The determination of the early Christians to continue in the apostles' doctrine and fellowship in that order (Acts 2:42)—was one secret of the unity they did enjoy. However, again and again we have seen intolerance towards the more conservative Christians—especially on the part of long-established Christian institutions such as the so-called Christian Universities—that augurs ill for the future of that great body of protesting and non-cooperating believers world-wide. Evangelical Christians often have to meet off the premises of 'Christian' institutions. If the colleges *were* essentially Christian they should welcome any such effort to win more for Christ. On the contrary, to preserve an apparent 'Christian' unity, they are content with lifeless formalism, knowing nothing of that unity in diversity which has been the secret of the Church's growth.

This oppressed group Billy Graham referred to when addressing the W.C.C. meeting in New Delhi, saying, 'This Assembly should not overlook the fact that there already exists within the Church a true ecumenical movement, which crosses all denominational, national and social barriers—an ecumenicity that proceeds from a common faith in the Christ of the Scriptures, of history and of personal experience . . .'

However it is becoming increasingly plain, as an I.F.E.S. report has pointed out, that 'ecumenism is a confused subject, the darling of both spiritual and unspiritual men, the tool of Communists as well as Jesuits, of self-seeking modern Diotrophes as well as John the Beloved.'

Ecumenical leaders of the calibre of Bishop Bergraav assure us that they feel God is too great a lover of variety to desire one great monolithic undifferentiated Protestant Church, and that he himself has no desire to see it. Dr Eugene Carson Blake once challenged fellow Presbyterians to be the best Presbyterians they could be—as being the best contribution to the ecumenical movement. Bishop Leslie Newbigin, one of the most conservative of the W.C.C. leaders, reminded one of their conferences of the fact that missionaries sent out by churches belonging to the W.C.C. were a decreasing proportion of the total force.

Whatever factors may be in favour of erasing ecclesiastical barriers and merging church orders, Norman Vincent Peale has pointed out that mergers inevitably lead to the concentration of power in fewer hands. It is for this very reason that many fear the autonomy of the local church is in grave danger in the face of the pretensions of a catholic and Reformed Church—a church which its leaders say must of necessity be hierarchical in government. The bishops will depart even further from their scriptural antecedents. The Pope of Rome has some justification for saying that the Protestant Church is walking towards him!

Not the least of the unfortunate possible effects of this grand effort at merger and uniformity is described very succinctly by Dr Charles Poling in his address on 'No Place to Hide', for he says, 'It is a simple but scientifically proven fact that the greater the mass the greater the inertia.'

The late Dr Samuel Zwemer was prophet enough to discern the possible effects of this movement on the outreach of the Church, warning us of the danger even in his day of identifying the term ecumenics with missions. 'The former is often of the mind; the latter of the heart. We may lift up our eyes and be ecumenical, but we must lift up our feet to be missionary. Missions are therefore the basis of true ecumenics and not ecumenics the basis of missions. Missions have made the Church ecumenical, but will ecumenics make the Church or an individual missionary? Does it produce prayer meetings?'

He foresaw what Billy Graham could challenge the W.C.C. with at New Delhi, namely, that over 60 per cent of the missionaries from America were outside the national Church.

We do well therefore to be sensitive to the aims and methods of the World Church movement, and to appreciate what is good and positive in its massive relief programmes and the softening periphery relationships with the Roman Catholic Church that makes for an increasing opportunity for the preaching of the Gospel in places previously unreachable. At the same time we cannot help but be saddened by the superficial definitions of what constitutes biblical unity and the nature of the Church itself.

In a wider sphere, the lack of discernment among Evangelicals of the true nature of the body of Christ has implications which also pose a grave problem, for it actually *attacks* the essential unity of the Church. It was just this fault for which Paul rebuked the Corinthian Christians in 1 Corinthians 11. His main theme in this passage is the unity of the Church, the body of Christ (see verses 17–19). The Corinthians needed to be reminded that they were not 'discerning the body' (verse 29), for with their personality-cults they were causing foolish divisions among themselves. They were failing to recognise, as Paul had previously pointed out to them in 10:17, that they all have to partake of one loaf; Christ cannot be divided.

It concerns me very little that there are so-called sects in the Church today, for there can still be a very real unity in the richest diversity. A number of churches or denominations have substantial reasons for existing as distinct units, for their national origins are different and they minister to a certain distinct culture. Some stem from what has been a greatly-needed revival in the past, and now the church in that branch could possibly do with another! From time to time, an outpouring of the Spirit can produce renewal and new protesting groups in the face of the general tendency to decadence. Indeed, it has been agreed that a church incapable of proliferation is dead. Certainly, if those who advocate a world Church increase their pressure for uniformity, it could be the Holy Spirit will render these efforts ineffective by spontaneous and irresistible lay movements breaking out from within.

The matter for real concern, however, is the quite unnecessary divisions caused by Pharasaism among us as Evangelicals. We make shades of doctrine that are incidental to saving faith into creeds fundamental to church membership. We tithe the mint, dill and cummin of traditional biblicism and neglect the weightier matters of utter reality, such as heart-to-heart oneness and obedience to the Holy Spirit through His Word.

Though we may be critical of the ecumenical movement, we do well to ask ourselves if we are enjoying the unity that is rightly ours. We certainly have the apostolic basis for unity, but it is one thing to cleave to a truly biblical faith and often another to revel in true heart oneness. The unity of the body is kept only at the cost of constant vigilance and no little warfare. It is like the peace which can only be preserved at the cost of a monumental preparation for war.

Doctrinal purity alone is not enough. Diotrephes was probably sound in faith, but even if he was never radical in theology he was radical enough in the pursuit of personal aggrandisement. His kind did not die with him. Neither is the unity of the body discerned only by those who are determined to preserve their little segment of it from the rest of Christendom. The more self-contained the group is, the more subject it is to 'popery'. Paul in Galatians 1:2 spoke of the churches in Judea, Luke describes the church in Judea and Samaria (Acts 9:31) without doubt meaning the various scattered assemblies of believers which Paul severally called 'churches'. Both concepts are true, which fact is often a comfort to me as I think of the little groups of lonely believers in some country areas of Japan, who probably have a real sense of being part of *the* body of Christ only when they meet occasionally with believers from the whole province.

One of the most encouraging things that has happened in modern times comes from Evangelism in Depth, where the total Christian force of a country is enlisted in an all-out effort to let every person know of Christ. The editor of *Decision* magazine has said, 'The Book of the Acts shows precisely how Christian unity can be obtained; by a God-centred, Spirit-filled, hell-raiding programme of evangelism. "Churches", said Lord Macleod, "are like steel, they come together only at white heat." '

Believers in the modern outreach of the Church militant in South America and Indonesia are experiencing in fullest measure the significance of a church life that revels in and expects to see every believer exercising the gifts of the Spirit. Leaders from Indonesia tell us of the lay evangelistic teams in which pastors sometimes take part but are not necessarily chosen as the leaders. The choice is made only after the group has come to oneness of mind about it through much prayer. This kind of fellowship in the Spirit and oneness of purpose that eclipses every secondary issue is born in the pursuit of evangelism. There is little room for the problems that dog the congregations where the passion for bringing people to Christ has gone.

How unity is attacked
The early church with all its outgoing zeal still had its unity attacked. First of all it was by the status-seekers Ananias and Sapphira, whose hypocrisy was unmasked only by sensitive Peter (Acts 5:1–11). He could discern by the Spirit what was foreign to the body of Christ and was willing to be the instrument for its expulsion.

Subsequent attacks followed alternatively from within and from without, as though Satan were equally at home with suitable strategy in either place, and tried one after another with increasing frustration. The next attack left the apostles badly bruised in body but far from beaten in spirit (Acts 5:40). It was probably more easily repulsed than the disunity caused by apparent partiality in distributing the alms (Acts 6:1–6). They wisely removed the cause of friction by giving a number of the Greek-background believers something to do which resulted in the choice of Stephen, who was soon to seal his zeal for the Saviour in blood.

And so the attacks proceeded and became more physically violent on the outside, but more sophisticated on the inside. Later, even in a church as healthy as that of the Philippians, we find two noble women who very decidedly did not discern the body, for their feud must have been common knowledge and a serious threat to that church's witness. Euodia and Syntyche had been fellow-labourers with Paul (Phil. 4:2, 3) and therefore were probably of equal zeal and ability, but for some reason they could not endure each other. This situation to my mind is more basic to the problem of the Church's unity than all the denominational issues put together.

Experience over the years leads us to make several suggestions as to why this could have occurred, for human nature has not changed. The problem of incompatible workers on the mission field is more grievous than in the home church for there is less room to escape from one another—unless one goes home! Sadly enough, sometimes both have to go home, for it plays havoc with their ministry and their health, not to mention that of those who try to make them amicable to each other.

It may just have been a simple matter of temperamental differences, and these can be distressing enough. I can see Barnabas and Paul working together but I just cannot imagine Paul and Peter working together! They can respect and love one another, as Peter did Paul, even though he had rebuked him publicly (2 Pet. 3:15), but it would be foolish waste to try to make two men like that work together. It is possible for us, if we have learned to laugh at ourselves and our foibles, honestly to recognise factors that make for incompatibility with others and so deliberately avoid unnecessary friction. Fellowship in the broad sense, yes, but the foot does not need to act like the hand or the body go on all fours— except when it is to play with the children!

Of course, the two women in question may have suffered from jealousy over who was really doing the most for Paul and then carried it over into later congregational life, not having forgotten the unintentional slights, or perhaps the gentle ribbing in the humorous Euodia that had too much of a cutting edge for the over-sensitive Syntyche. The slights could be given a male-volent twist by well-intentioned husbands, but basic to it all would be the lack of control of the tongue and the heart condition that makes it wag (Mark 7:21-3). Having myself been guilty of remarks for which later I could have bitten off my tongue, I have often given silent testimony to the truth of James's assertion that the person who can control his tongue is perfect indeed (Jas. 3:2). If Euodia and Syntyche could both have been silent among their respective coterie of friends, then the winds of gossip would have had none of those gossamer-like seeds of half-truth, bitterness and misunderstanding to blow to unretrievable areas of influence for evil.

Paul's rebuke about not discerning the body was directed at the Corinthians in the very simple setting of the Lord's supper and 'agape' or love-feast. Theirs was a lack of courtesy—a lack of good table-manners, if you like. There was greed, thoughtlessness, class distinction and self-indulgence—in short, ethical problems that had a far-reaching theological impact. The feast was meant to be a simple but telling symbol of the fact that we were not only reconciled to God by the death of His Son but that same death had broken down dividing walls between race and race, class and class, and between individuals at conflict with one another.

What brings friction and dismemberment to the body of Christ so often is not some grave theological issue, a radical difference in the way Christian work is done, or the lack of comity between bludgeoning new groups of evangelical causes. It is the simple, ethical problem of person-to-person relationships. One mission has blamed broken relationships for 59 per cent of the missionary failures. They have been unable to make a succussful adjustment to fellow-workers or to mission authority.

Unless there is a daily adorning of the doctrine of I Corinthians 13 in all these things, the close team-work in any Christian group will bring envy at another's success, misjudgment of another's motives, smugness at another's downfall, fear of loss of others' approval, lack of patience with and respect for those over us in the Lord, condescending patronage of others whom we think less gifted than ourselves, fierce assertiveness when we think our rights are denied or infringed upon, and grudges against others that are relished and nursed in the heart because self-pity is raucous in its claim for attention. While maintaining a façade of propriety to keep up with the 'in-group', there can be a gross worldliness in thought-life and action in the home, because we are 'fundamental' only by accident and not by burning conviction—that kind of burning that has left uneffaceable scars.

These to my mind are some of the factors that grieve the Holy Spirit in the midst of His people and destroy the spirit of prayer. This is evident enough when we think of the records of any mighty visitation of the Holy Spirit in revival. These are the things that suddenly have become unbearable in His searching light. Overwhelming grief at unlove towards others has led to transparent fellowship.

While we cannot manufacture a revival like this we can and must fight to maintain the unity that is already ours in Christ and fulfil the conditions that make for a full enjoyment of what it means to be a member of the body of Christ. It falls to leaders in particular to help others see this as a focal point of satanic attack, and at any personal cost to themselves, to set an example of a truly discerning spirit in the maintenance of unity.

12

The Enabling

Any Christian responsibility has a number of built-in perils. In some cultures, physical danger is of course the most apparent, for the frontiers of rising nationalism and militant materialism are often studded with the graves of men whose convictions and very influence in society marked them out for early extinction.

A more prosaic peril arises out of an unwise dissipation of energy. As leaders we do not clock in at a certain time and the Boss is never seen, but if we are sincere in our calling tremendous demands can be made upon our nervous energy. Dr A. W. Tozer argued that no preacher had a right to die of old age if hard work could kill him. Perhaps his own untimely death occurred for that very reason.

Obviously some, by natural temperament and physical stamina, can carry a tremendous work load. There seems to be a source of unquenchable enthusiasm that leaves the more phlegmatic of us far in the gasping rear. However, this surely should be distinguished from that inner fire generated by the Holy Spirit in the life of the person wholly yielded to Him. He can make the retiring disposition radiant even if it never becomes radical.

The balance between downright laziness and reckless

expenditure of energy is preserved for most of us mainly by force of circumstance. Given the ministry of a man like Evan Roberts, the Welsh revivalist of the early twentieth century, we might soon find ourselves, as he did, subject to nervous strain, which in his case abruptly terminated his ministry at the peak of its usefulness. Apparently doctors were consulted but no one seemed to be able to shield the leader of the revival from secondary issues, or direct him into a wise choice of priorities and the maintenance of adequate physical and nervous relaxation. Today's evangelists now know that the laws of health are as inexorable in their demands as are those of the Decalogue, and that we cannot despise one without influencing our ministry in the other!

To many of us, confrontation can be demanding enough and 'burn us up' more than the busiest preaching schedule ever will. True, some seem to delight in being the Lord's self-appointed watchdogs, for ever barking at the heels of the latest heretic or cause that might fool the gullible Christian public, but these are a peculiar few.

In Paul's case, one wonders if confrontation were not the issue that cost him the most. He closes his unbelievable catalogue of physical sufferings for Christ in 2 Corinthians 11:23–9 with what may appear a lame remark about his being indignant when someone is made to fall. Did his anxiety for the churches cost him more than an occasional back-beating as at the Philippian jail? Did not it cost more to rebuke Peter before the whole church when he momentarily defected to the Judaisers than it did to face a screaming mob in Jerusalem? Certainly to disagree with Barnabas over Mark must have cost him much more than to see the back of Demas. The subtle influence of false brethren, the opposition of leaders who disputed his apostleship, and the whispering campaign of those who maligned his intentions; these are the issues that sound the minor chord throughout most of his epistles.

For the convinced Christian, confrontation in some form or other is inevitable. The care of the churches today is no less demanding than it was in Paul's day, for though the issues usually appear less dramatic, they are none the less subtle. Today, too, we face the many-sided and ever-encroaching demands of a world Church, plus the exasperating and persistent zeal of false cults. Within the Church itself, there is a constant vacillation in theological opinion that taxes one's powers of discernment to the utmost and calls for the greatest firmness.

Perhaps the most common peril, however, is just the simple matter of enervation. It creeps up on us like old age. We become all too accustomed to a regular ministry. We cut a groove of sameness and threaten to lie down in it. Whether we wear the incriminating clerical garb or not, we are in danger of becoming mere professionals. The adventure goes, and human beings become mere clinical cases. There are 'no conversations, just conferences, no plain people like the Lord loved, but only "cases" and people with problems'.[1] The whole life, plus that greatly longed-for holiday at the sea to break the monotony, can become thoroughly institutionalised. The final tragedy is when we then welcome a theology that dulls the sense of accountability. These and many other related problems point up the leader's peculiar need of special enablement.

Paul's secret of enablement
Paul, both in his life and teaching, gives a satisfying answer to this need, and yet it is no simple answer. There is no single facet of his life nor one dominant theme in his teaching that gives the whole answer.

Looking at his life from the Godward side, you see the moments of ecstasy, the transports of heavenly delight, and the unearthly experiences that touched every accompanying weakness with glory. He was so obviously chosen of God to His high calling, and the Spirit of God had taken hold of him for a specific task. Yet from the manward side, no one has surpassed Paul for his utter dedication; his entire personality is like a constantly poured-out libation on the altar of other people's needs. On the one hand, therefore, Paul was conscious of being chosen to an apostleship and on the other he was the Lord's slave by willing and intelligent choice. In Romans 1:1 both aspects are one mouthful in the apostolic greeting.

Now, I know of no portion of Paul's writings where these two emphases are more satisfyingly treated and more embracing in their scope than in the First Letter to the Corinthians. Here we have unfolded in the moving drama of early church life the exquisite interplay between the sovereign control of the Spirit on the one hand, and the willing dedication of the mind, spirit, and body to His control on the other. We can look at each one of these aspects in turn.

The Holy Spirit and the mind
In 1 Corinthians 2:10–16 we are reminded that the Spirit enlightens our minds to understand the mysteries of God and the significance of the gifts He bestows. Apart from the Spirit, we cannot understand the mysteries of God, we cannot communicate God's wisdom to others, even of like faith, and we certainly cannot communicate life to those outside Christ. Then, not least, it is by the same Spirit that we are given discernment to judge whether or not the thing is truly of God.

All this on the surface places a decided stress on the Holy Spirit's control of our intellectual faculties; but at the same time there is no encouragement here for the vacant mind, and less still for the lazy one! Those of a certain school of thought despise learning and unwittingly would blame the Holy Spirit if upon opening their mouths nothing inspirational seemed to come out. Paul, on the other hand, could hardly be said to belittle the discipline of the study that sharpened his mind and filled his memory with material suited to the constant disputations and arguments whenever he sought to persuade the Jews (Acts 17:17; 18:4).

Nor does his claim to have the mind of Christ (1 Cor. 2:16) signify any strange possession or mystical superimposition of the Spirit's presence whereby Paul becomes a mere cipher or mouthpiece for divine utterance. Over the vexed marriage question dealt with in chapter 7 of the same letter, Paul hesitates to make any such claim, and we might well ask ourselves just how he could discern between speaking with the mind of Christ and merely giving his own personal opinion, for what it was worth, as an apostle (compare verses 10, 12, 25). Without giving way to theological gymnastics, or relegating this distinction wholly to the age of the apostles when special inspiration could be expected, we need as leaders to be so taught of the Spirit that we can indeed discern the Lord's mind—as distinct from our own.

D. E. Hoste tells of a conversation with Hudson Taylor, who confessed that whereas in his younger days things seemed to come so clearly and so quickly, now, as he had gone on and God had used him more and more, so often he seemed to be like a man going along in a fog.[2] No doubt when we are still young in the faith we are in need of the wind and the fire, the sensory stimuli that give distinctive and unmistakable point to the Spirit's leading, but after trial in the furnace of affliction and success, the still small voice of the Spirit is like a zephyr breeze upon our spirit and we need to be hidden in with Him to hear it.

In this same connection, the fullness of the Spirit does not call for a passive mind either. In the centre of the passage dealing with the vexed question of the unwise exercise of tongues in the Corinthian church (1 Cor. 14:20), Paul calls for maturity in thinking, for though he can speak in tongues more than them all (verses 18, 19) nevertheless he can so control the exercise of the gift that he prefers rather to instruct others with an intelligible tongue. In other words, our worship should never become irrational, and though in the course of worshipping Him with all our hearts we have an unsought experience of tongues or some other overpowering exhibition of His presence, we must seek to hold it within the wholesome bounds of scriptural order and certainly not demand an identical experience for all.

Jonathan Goforth of China, because of a profound dissatisfaction with his ministry, turned all his attention to a prolonged study of the person and work of the Spirit. He never confessed to any speaking in tongues, yet we know that the Lord did bless that disciplined study in a subsequent ministry of great fruitfulness and revival. Christian biography, if nothing else, reveals a striking dissimilarity when it comes to any manifest initial and felt work of the Spirit in fullness upon His children. Both Finney and Moody could be said to have had such overpowering experiences of the Spirit's presence that on occasion it was declared to be almost unbearable. Contrast this with the quiet and yet far-reaching decision of a man like F. B. Meyer to enter into all that the Spirit had for him, with evident revolutionary changes in his subsequent fruitful ministry. So whether the initial encounter with the Spirit in fullness has been an emotional upheaval of unearthly proportions, or simply an unspectacular but desperately real grasp of God's promises, there has never been a deliberate attempt *not* to use the mind, as is advocated by some. Judging by the safeguards Paul gives for the public use of the gifts of tongues and of prophecy, he expects the mind to be fully employed.

In the description of the various gifts of the Spirit, the ability to distinguish between spirits is sandwiched in between the gift of prophecy and that of various kinds of tongues (1 Cor. 12 : 10). It is an ability not a gift, but certainly a manifestation of the Spirit (verse 7), and even if acquired, presumably subject to development. That non-Christians and the demon-possessed can also speak in tongues should be noted. Such manifestations appear in some heathen religions.[3]

Because of the phenomenal rise of occultism these days, I feel that the discerning of spirits is very much needed. For this reason I wrote to a missionary friend in Indonesia who I know has had a valuable experience in this sphere, asking his opinion as to how the ability operates in actual practice. He replied to the effect that:

> (a) It enables the Lord's servant to discover the presence of the occult in a person who is actively using satanic powers.
>
> (b) It enables the Lord's servant to discover Satan's control of a person who has passively used demonic powers, i.e. for healing, for protection and for success etc.
>
> (c) It enables the Lord's servant to differentiate between demonic possession and mental illness, or where both are present.
>
> (d) It enables the Lord's servant to understand if there is occult heritage behind certain evil features of character which binds a person, or temporary possession by certain evil spirits such as uncleanness, anger etc.
>
> (e) It enables the Lord's servant to discern if a so-called spiritual ministry is carried out by the Spirit or in the realm and faculties of the soul alone.
>
> (f) It enables the Lord's servant to detect evil spirits in a house or in a room.

He also gave what he thought were some tangible signs of what could be expected if the person concerned has been engaged in occultism either passively or actively. He suggested that the person for instance will fall asleep against his own will when listening to the Word of God. He will be hard and unresponsive to the Gospel. He will be unable to pray. He will not want to read the Word of God. He will hate any mention of the blood of

Christ and become restless when it is talked about. He will perhaps curse the Name of Jesus. There will be attacks of depression. Some have been known to be temporarily paralysed bodily for a time. There have been visions during the night when dead people are said to appear, and the intention to commit suicide is not uncommon.

The more common situation for the exercise of discernment would be no doubt in the regular church-worship service. Some principles are clearly given as to how to encourage the biblical exercise of these gifts. For instance does the use of the gift make for the common good (1 Cor. 12:7)? Because the gift tends to be spectacular is it occupying too prominent a place in public worship (12:28–31)? In the exercise of the gift publicly am I striving to build up the church (1 Cor. 14:12)? Am I mature enough (14:20) to agree with Paul that it is better to speak five intelligible words that will instruct, than ten thousand that no-one can understand (14:19)? If the constraint to speak in tongues is there, do I intelligently recognise the need of an interpreter for the message before I indulge in the expression of them publicly (14:27)? Am I so in control of my own spirit, mentally speaking, that whatever my gift is, the exercise of it makes for peace and not for confusion (14:33)?

The Holy Spirit and our spirits
In 1 Corinthians 2:11, 12, Paul touches upon a relationship between the Holy Spirit and our own spirit that is very difficult to define. In 5:4 Paul could speak of his spirit being present in a distant gathering as a powerful motivating moral force in a local church situation calling for the sternest discipline. Later (6:17) he speaks of the vital union of our spirits with the Holy Spirit, and in 7:34 assures us that holiness is possible for both body and spirit.

Surely our own spirit is where the Holy Spirit is Himself active at the core of our being. There we are made alive by His presence and we are flooded with love by His gracious fullness (Rom. 5:5). Paul's famous poem to love in 1 Corinthians 13 is the final answer to the most constructive use of the gifts that are described in chapter 12. In other words, the fruit of the Spirit is safe-guarded against the abuse of the gifts of the Spirit. For example, Paul is careful to speak of patience as the in-dubitable proof, alongside the signs, wonders, and mighty works, of his being an apostle (2 Cor. 12:12). The moral must balance the miraculous.

Indeed, in the practical day-by-day problems of Chris-tian living, the moral issues offer the supreme test of reality and Spirit-fullness. Am I prepared to pay the cost of transparent fellowship? Am I sweetly reasonable in the face of misunderstanding and misrepresentation? Am I sympathetically awake to the unspoken needs of others? Is there an uncalculating love that plans the best and thinks the best for all I touch? Is there spontaneous praise even when God seems to contradict Himself and circumstances cause me to cry aloud in self-pity? Only as we yield to the Holy Spirit is He able to take up each new circumstance and in the crucible of daily experi-ence forge into our very spirits a Christ-likeness which is obviously easier to describe than to practise.

It has been pointed out that the fruit of the Spirit is love, joy, peace, longsuffering, gentleness, goodness, faith, meekness, and temperance *combined*. For that reason, in one sense 1 Corinthians 13 is a commentary upon them all, for these are all but facets of God's love at work in our hearts, and Christian living without this kind of love is difficult indeed.

The Holy Spirit and our bodies
Finally, the Holy Spirit is said to dwell in our bodies as His temple. This is one of the most deeply motivating forces in a Christian leader's life. Paul argues for an awareness of this upon the Corinthian believers who were specially subject to loose sexual relationships. Our

body, like money, is a wonderful slave, but it makes a very poor master. Paul, therefore, devotes 1 Corinthians 6:9–20, with verse 19 as a pivotal point, to the problem of the Christian's control of his body, and in 9:24 sums up his attitude towards his body in words that indicate an unrelenting battle.

The Rev. George B. Duncan, in his helpful treatment of the fullness of the Spirit, had a chapter on 'The Disciplines That Must be Managed'. He writes:

> It is so often a lack of discipline which fails to allow the Holy Spirit to do that in us for which He has been given. It may be discipline of time that is lacking, or, perhaps, a discipline of our thought; and it is here that the relationship between grace and what we call the 'means of grace' comes in. It is here that we see the relationship between faith and effort. We cannot create the fullness of the Spirit, but we can condition it. We have the Holy Spirit, but we can grieve Him by failing to allow Him to work in us that for which He has been given. Fail here and you fail everywhere. You fail because the Holy Spirit is grieved in your life. In this connection, I think it is true to say that the disciplines that we must manage are usually the disciplines that are unseen. The secret of spiritual fullness seldom has a public audience. If you meet a man in whose life this condition is being maintained, you find a Christian in whom the ministries of the Spirit of God—keep it clear, the ministries, not gifts, of the Spirit—are being fulfilled; if you come across a man like that, you will find that in his life or in her life there is an absolutely iron discipline . . .[4]

The body, of course, does respond beneficially to the stimulus of the Lord's joy in our hearts—it becomes our strength indeed. Our whole body and related nervous system is toned up as it were by a clear-cut demanding vision of the world's need and our part in meeting it, but a study of Paul's Spirit-filled life will also point up the fact that, though he evidently revelled in every needed gift and displayed the graces of the Spirit's presence, there were times when he despaired of life, when he was cast down even if he was never knocked out, when he could long for physical wholeness to the extent of being refused healing three times. Such were his involuntary trials, there were times when, if it were not for the needs of others still young in the faith, he would fain have been delivered from the body altogether.

The pivotal point referred to in 1 Corinthians 6:19 is of course a challenge to recognise the holy character of the Guest whom we entertain, in whose presence any physical relationship outside the will of God should be intolerable. This for Paul was the realm of voluntary trial as it is for us. In this day when the privileged West needs to apologise to Sodom and Gomorrah for not being violently overthrown in spite of the enormity of its sexual vices, the Christian leader specially needs to set a decided example in his relationship with the other sex. It is hardly possible to err here on the side of carefulness for it is all too easy to give the wrong impression even when we are engaged in personal evangelism! Some Christian leaders have lost their reputation, some their positions in Christian society, through lack of wisdom in this regard.

Discipline and the Spirit's fullness
The fullness of the Holy Spirit is a must for the responsible Christian. It is a command to be obeyed (Eph. 5:18), and a privilege to be enjoyed. It is not a once-for-all experience that will deprive us of the necessity of repeated fillings nor of the need of special unction for special occasions. Neither are the fruits of the Spirit automatically manifested. It calls on our part for a whole-hearted choosing of His will, and for a loathing of what is foreign to His holy nature in mind, spirit and

body. There will need to be self-imposed discipline.

There will be the discipline of the mind: the storing of the mind with the Word of God (Col. 3 : 16). There will be the discipline of the spirit: exercising faith regardless of how I feel; the fact of the indwelling Holy Spirit can be demonstrated in acts of positive outgoing faith. There will be the disciplining of the body. It can be helpful on occasion to offer up our bodies part by part to the Spirit's control and fullness.

There appears to be no one formula common to the needs and opportunities of us all. He 'divides', not only His gifts, but the manifest token of His presence as He will, and this makes for much of the adventure and richness of the Christian life. 'The fire of God's anointing for service falls only upon a sacrifice', and it is obviously the kind of sacrifice that it is more difficult to *be* than to *offer*. Wherever these disciplines are exercised, however, it will result increasingly in the Lordship of Christ, for the fullness of the Spirit *is* the Lordship of Christ. It was for *that* reason He was given.

1. A. W. Tozer, in an article entitled 'Dangers for the Preacher'.

2. See Phyllis Thompson, *D. E. Hoste* (Overseas Missionary Fellowship), p. 131.

3. See Homer Dowdy, *Christ's Witchdoctor* (Hodder and Stoughton).

4. George B. Duncan, *Be Filled with the Spirit* (Inter-Varsity Press), pp. 10–11.

IMPACT BOOKS

Amazing Grace

Marcus L. Loane

A series of studies throwing light on particular aspects of St Paul's spiritual experience, facets of his unique ministry and his apostolic testimony. To understand more fully the meaning of Paul's writings, Marcus Loane looks at the passages selected with careful reference to the context of their original meaning.

Studies in the letter to the Hebrews are included in this volume to present a well-rounded series of studies which epitomise the wholesome and instructive coverage we have come to expect from Dr Loane's Bible studies.

Current books by Marcus L. Loane, Archbishop of Sydney, include:

THE HILL OF THE CROSS *Lakeland* 117

JOHN THE BAPTIST *Lakeland* 214

Evangelism—
The Counter-Revolution

Lewis A. Drummond

Essential aspects of evangelism in the context of the local church. A lively and growing concern for Christian outreach characterises this topical study in mission and evangelism. Lewis Drummond is an American Baptist, whose present appointment at Spurgeon's College, London, has enabled him fully to understand the situation in Britain; he has also travelled widely and met evangelists and church leaders from many countries at international conferences.

After fifteen years in pastoral work (including a church with 3,000 membership in Louisville, Kentucky) Dr Drummond affirms that the local church must be the focal point for sustained evangelism. He speaks not only to ministers and leaders but to every committed Christian, showing how a more effective witness may be given in this revolutionary age.

The World's Greatest Sermon

J. Oswald Sanders

A devotional verse-by-verse exposition of the Sermon on the Mount, this new work by Oswald Sanders is characteristically profound in its understanding. A comprehensive introduction covers the background of the sermon, throws light on Christ's teaching and guides the reader towards a correct interpretation. There follows a detailed study which both preachers and laymen will find illuminating, inspiring and instructive.

J. Oswald Sanders, the widely-travelled former General Director of the Overseas Missionary Fellowship (C.I.M.) is the author of a dozen books which have a world-wide ministry, including:

THE HOLY SPIRIT AND HIS GIFTS
THE INCOMPARABLE CHRIST
MEN FROM GOD'S SCHOOL
HERESIES AND CULTS *Lakeland* 138
SPIRITUAL LEADERSHIP *Lakeland* 191